# The Believer's School of Training

# MINISTERING in the POWER of the HOLY of the SPIRIT

"And the yoke shall be destroyed because of the anointing" *Isaiah 10:27*

*A Teaching Syllabus Equipping Believers to Move In New Testament Ministry by the Anointing of the Holy Spirit*

# NORMAN ROBERTSON

*Ministering in the Power of the Holy Spirit*

© 1994 by Norman Robertson

P.O. Box 3330

Matthews, North Carolina 28106 USA

ISBN 0-9636898-2-7

Printed in the United States of America

NRM Publications

P.O. Box 3330

Matthews, North Carolina 28106

# MINISTERING in the POWER HOLY of the SPIRIT

## by
## Norman
## Robertson

NRM Publications
P.O. Box 3330
Matthews, North Carolina 28106
(704) 847-5999 telephone
(704) 845-9365 fax

# The Teaching Library of Norman Robertson

Norman Robertson Ministries
P.O. Box 3330
Matthews, NC 28106
(704) 847-5999

## AUDIO TAPES

**Two-tape albums**
- Living Under an Open Heaven
- Christ the Healer
- Knowing the Person of the Holy Spirit
- Stirring Up the Gifts of the Holy Spirit
- Healing From Heaven
- The Guiding Voice of the Holy Spirit
- Financial Increase
- Making Your Way Prosperous
- Flowing in the Anointing

**Three-tape albums**
- The Holy Spirit—Who He Is and What He Does
- The Ministry of Divine Healing

**Six-Tape Albums**
- The Supernatural Church
- Ministering in the Power of the Holy Spirit

**Single Audio Cassette Tapes**
- Anointed for Action
- Victory in Your Finances
- Faith for Healing
- Various Selected Sermons

## BOOKS

- The Supernatural Church
- Winners in Christ
- Tithing
- Ministering in the Power of the Holy Spirit
- Improving Your Love Life
- Walking in Victory

**To contact the author, write:**
Norman Robertson
P.O. Box 3330
Matthews, North Carolina 28106
(704) 847-5999 telephone
(704) 845-9365 fax

It is important to us that we continue ministering to you and helping you to grow spiritually. We have a library of anointed teaching materials that will help you develop in your Christian life.

New products are being released regularly, so for a complete list of our ministry products, **write, call,** or **fax** our ministry office today!

# Table
# of
# Contents

*"Forwarded with permission"*

WORD OF GOD MINISTRIES
*Bob & Jean Shaw*
14439 S. Highway 259
Leitchfield, KY  42754

Phone/Fax:  270-257-8980

# *Introduction*

**Dear Student of God's Word,**

## 2 Timothy 3:16,17

Welcome to *The Believer's School of Training*!

The course of study you have chosen will be extremely beneficial to your spiritual development in becoming the dynamic new testament disciple God intended you to be. Allow the Holy Spirit to be your teacher and guide as you study the lessons each week on this vital subject, "Ministering in the Power of the Holy Spirit."

The successful completion of your studies will involve these four basic essentials - decision, discipline, diligence, and determination. Therefore, do not allow people, circumstances, the devil, or your flesh to keep you from spending quality time in study each week. You can do it, and my prayer for you is Ephesians 1:17-22

The revelation instruction in this new testament training program will challenge, edify, inform, and motivate you to start doing the works of Jesus by allowing God in you to meet the needs of people around you.

**My personal advice to you:**

1. Begin each study lesson with prayer, asking the Holy Spirit to guide you and give you understanding.

2. Do not work too quickly. Take time to read, study, and meditate on each of the truths you are learning.

3. Mark your Bible with the verses in the lessons and make personal notes as God speaks to you and gives you revelation knowledge.

4. Pay special attention to the section "Response to Truth" and answer all of the self-check questions.

5. Above all, be determined to be a doer of God's word—not only a hearer. Life application is vital to your spiritual growth.

6. Be committed to a New Testament local church and make yourself available to your pastor to support his vision for reaching your community

7. Stay on the cutting-edge with a program of continuous learning and self development — order our other workbooks, audio tapes and ministry materials from our teaching library.

God Bless You!

*Norman Robertson*

Dr. Norman Robertson

# LESSON: 1           The Power of Pentecost

**PERSONAL NOTES**

**KEY VERSE:**      Acts 3:19      *"Repent therefore and be converted, that your sins may be blotted out, so that times of refreshing may come from the presence of the Lord."*

**KEY TRUTH:**      We live in a hostile, humanistic society which is resistant to the Gospel. People need to see and experience God and His power working today in their midst.

**KEY SCRIPTURES:**   John 14, 15, 16; Acts 1:8; Acts 2:16-18; Acts 2:38, 39; Acts 3:19-21; Acts 10:44; 1 Thessalonians 1:5; Hebrews 2:4

The New Testament clearly reveals that the miraculous was never intended to disappear from the church, rather God's supernatural power will increase more and more until Jesus returns.

## OUTPOURING OF THE HOLY SPIRIT AT PENTECOST

On the day of Pentecost, when the 120 disciples together in one accord had prayed, fasted, and waited upon God for ten days in the upper room, the Holy Spirit fell upon them suddenly, clothing them, baptizing them, empowering them. The overwhelming experience of being filled with the Holy Spirit brought the manifestation of speaking in other tongues; which got the attention of the people of Jerusalem.

The Jews asked, "What does this mean? Are these men drunk?"

Peter got up and preached an anointed sermon, quoting from the Prophet Joel and his prophecy about the last days.

Acts 2:16-19

The Bible says that Pentecost marked the beginning of the last days. The church today is living in the last of the last days — possibly in the last hour.

Notice what was prophesied about the move of the Holy Spirit in the last days.

### NUMBER 1

*"In the last days I will pour out My Spirit on all flesh."*

God's Word predicts an increase of the supernatural outpouring of the Holy Spirit in the last days - "UPON ALL FLESH." (All flesh means Black, White, Saved, Unsaved, Irish, Asian, North American, Pentecostal, Lutheran, Methodist, Dutch Reform, etc.).

This speaks of a great increase of salvations plus an increase of believers being baptized in the Holy Spirit.

God's end time revival involves a supernatural outpouring of the Holy Spirit that will touch and affect all nations as well as denominations.

# The Power of Pentecost

**PERSONAL NOTES**

## NUMBER 2

*"Your sons and your daughters shall prophesy."*

This speaks of the move of the Holy Spirit among young people. There is coming a great revival among teenagers and the youth.

## NUMBER 3

*"Your young men shall see visions, your old men shall dream dreams."*

This speaks about the increase of spiritual manifestations in the last days.

## NUMBER 4

*"On My menservants (five-fold ministry) and on My maidservants (women in ministry) I will pour out My Spirit in those days."*

This speaks about the increase of the anointing coming upon the five-fold ministry gifts in the last days.

## NUMBER 5

*"And they (God's servants/five-fold ministry) shall prophesy."*

This speaks about an increase in prophetic ministry in the last days – the gift of prophecy will be in greater manifestation.

## NUMBER 6

*"I will show wonders in heaven above and signs in the earth beneath."*

This prophecy for the last days proclaims that there will be a greater manifestation of signs, wonders, miracles, and gifts of the Holy Spirit.

When is the timing of this six-fold prophecy?

**Acts 2:17** says **the last days.**

**Acts 2:20** says **before the return of Jesus.**

Child of God, we must realize that God gave the gift of the Holy Spirit on the day of Pentecost and He has been on the earth ever since.

- The Holy Spirit is here, and now pouring out His anointing upon all flesh.

- The Holy Spirit is on the earth today continuing the "ministry of Jesus" through teaching, preaching, healing, and manifesting signs, wonders and miracles.

- The Holy Spirit is always present to confirm, endorse, and demonstrate the message of God's Word.

- The Holy Spirit comes into our meetings and manifests Himself when we ask Him.

**Luke 11:13**

- He comes to **change** and **charge** the atmosphere with his anointing.

# The Power of Pentecost

- He comes to manifest the works of Jesus.

- He comes to release His supernatural gifts.

- He comes to pour out His presence.

*"Where the spirit is Lord there is liberty."*          2 Corinthians 3:17 (Greek)

We need to HONOR the Holy Spirit, give Him pre-eminence and lordship in our worship services, and allow Him to move and manifest His presence and power.

## OUTPOURING OF THE HOLY SPIRIT IN THE BOOK OF ACTS

Acts 11:21                 Acts 14:3                 Acts 15:12

(1)  Peter's anointed preaching on the day of Pentecost caused 3,000 people to be born again and follow Jesus.

Acts 2:41

(2)  The crippled beggar at the temple gate received a miracle healing as Peter spoke the name of Jesus.

Acts 3:1-8, 16

(3)  The mass healing of multitudes in the streets of Jerusalem took place because the anointing radiated from Peter's shadow.

Acts 5:12, 15, 16

(4)  Stephen moved in signs and wonders anointed by the Holy Spirit.

Acts 6:8

(5)  Philip, the deacon, held a great revival in Samaria with powerful preaching followed by miraculous signs which caused the whole city to be touched by the anointing of God.

Acts 8:5-8

(6)  The Holy Spirit fell upon Cornelius and the Gentiles causing them to be born again and baptized in the Spirit.

Acts 10:44-46

(7)  By the anointing of the Holy Spirit, Paul cast the spirit of fortune-telling out of a demon possessed woman. (Compare this with the ministry of Jesus – Luke 11:20).

Acts 16:16-18

(8)  By the anointing of the Holy Spirit, special miracles, signs, and wonders manifested through the hands of Paul.

Acts 19:11, 12

# The Power of Pentecost

© 1994 The Believer's School of Training, Rev. Norman K. Robertson

## OUTPOURING OF THE HOLY SPIRIT IN THE CHURCH AGE

### Revivals of the past 300 years:

* John Wesley, George Whitfield, Jonathan Edwards, Charles Finney, D. L. Moody, Mrs. Woodworth Etter, John Alexander Dowie, John G. Lake

### In the 20th Century

| | | |
|---|---|---|
| 1901 | Topeka Kansas: Outpouring and baptism in the Holy Spirit. | Charles F. Parham |
| 1904 | Welsh Revival | Evan Roberts |
| 1906 | Azuza Street Revival, Los Angeles. Three and one half years non-stop revival causing a pentecostal explosion around the world. | William "Daddy" Seymour |
| 1947 – 1959 | Divine healing revival in USA. Laying on of hands restored. Miracle ministries raised up. | William Branham A. A. Allen Jack Coe Oral Roberts Latter Rain Movement |
| 1960's – 1970's | Charismatic Renewal–Outpouring and baptism in the Holy Spirit touches mainline churches and all denominations. | Kathryn Kuhlman Miracle Services |
| 1970's – 1980's | Revival of teaching God's Word – emphasis on Word of Faith, healing, prosperity. | Kenneth Hagin Fred Price Norvel Hayes Kenneth Copeland Jerry Savelle, etc. |
| 1980's | Mega Churches raised up such as Rhema South Africa and Lakewood Church, Houston, Texas. | Ray McCauley John Osteen |

1980's (cont.)

Morris Cerullo miracle crusades and global evangelism/schools of ministry.

Dr. Yonggi Cho – Home Cell System influences the Body of Christ.

Mass Evangelism in Africa – Reinhard Bonnke preaching to ten million souls each year.

John Wimber, Vineyard Ministries' emphasis on the Kingdom of God equips evangelical churches to move in signs and wonders.

Larry Lea's emphasis on prayer as the key to revival for the body of Christ.

Praise, worship, and prophetic ministry emphasized.

1990's    Benny Hinn mass miracle healing crusades in USA and Europe. Evangelist Rodney Howard-Browne stirring the church with Holy Ghost Revival – signs and wonders.

# The Power of Pentecost

This period begins the fulfillment of the great outpouring of the Holy Spirit prophesied by Smith Wigglesworth in the early 1940's, emphasizing the Ministry of the Word and the Ministry of Spirit.

## 1990's to the Rapture of the Church

A mighty, Holy Spirit revival will continue to spread throughout the USA, Europe, and touch many nations.

Corporate anointing coming upon the whole church, believers in the body of Christ will rise up and take their rightful place of ministry in the great commission and go out and do the works of Jesus.

## OUTPOURING OF THE HOLY SPIRIT IN THE LAST DAYS

What things can we expect ahead for the church?

There is coming a LAST DAY outpouring of the Holy Spirit which will be like a **tidal wave** of revival combining all that has happened from Acts, throughout church history until the present day.

(1) We will enter a higher dimension of praise and worship that will manifest the corporate anointing in our churches as never before.

> Acts 4:24-31
> 2 Chronicles 5:13, 14

(2) We will see a supernatural increase in evangelism harvesting millions of souls, and an explosion of church growth we have not seen before.

> Acts 11:21

(3) We will see a deeper desire and love for the Word of God as never before.

> Amos 8:11

(4) We will receive a greater ability to destroy the works of the devil, and supernaturally minister to the needs of people.

> Luke 4:18

Put this fact in your spirit today — demons are not on the increase but Holy Ghost people are.

(5) There will be a greater spirit of giving and a new financial stewardship upon the church in the last days so that the end time revival can be financed.

> Deuteronomy 8:18
> Matthew 24:14

(6) We will see an explosion of Holy Spirit power greater than in the Book of Acts, manifesting notable miracles, signs, and wonders including creative miracles.

> Romans 15:18, 19
> 1 Corinthians 4:20
> Hebrews 2:4

*"...the people who know their God shall be strong, and carry out great exploits."*

> Daniel 11:32

# The Power of Pentecost

© 1994 The Believer's School of Training, Rev. Norman K. Robertson

**PERSONAL NOTES**

*"Your God has commanded your strength; Strengthen, O God, what You have done for us."*

**Psalm 68:28**

Kathryn Kuhlman said:

"The day is coming, before Jesus returns, when every sick saint in the body of Christ will be healed – there will be services where every single sick person in the building will be healed by the power of God."

In **Luke 19:13 (KJV)**, Jesus commands His church to "occupy" until He comes. **The word "occupy" implies more than a passive resistance. It refers to a militant occupying force, boldly enforcing the rule of the conquering King.**

Our job is
- to WIN the world for Jesus
- to IMPACT COMMUNITIES with the Gospel
- to actively carry out Mark 16

## STIRRING UP THE ANOINTING

*"Behold, I send the Promise of my Father upon you; but tarry in the city of Jerusalem until you are endued with power from on high."*
**Luke 24:49**

*"Most assuredly, I say to you, he who believes in Me, the works that I do he will do also; and greater works than these he will do, because I go to My Father."*
**John 14:12**

*"How God anointed Jesus of Nazareth with the Holy Spirit and with power, who went about doing good and healing all who were oppressed by the devil, for God was with Him."*
**Acts 10:38**

*"As You sent Me into the world, I also have sent them into the world."*
**John 17:18**

*"That is why I would remind you to stir up – rekindle the embers, fan the flame and keep burning– the [gracious] gift of God, [the inner fire] that is in you."*
**2 Timothy 1:6 (AMP)**

**How do we stir up the anointing and gifts of the Spirit?**
How do we stir up the supernatural power of God?
(1) By praising and worshipping Him.
(2) By daily studying and meditating on the miracles, signs, and wonders in the four Gospels and in the Book of Acts.
(3) By praying much in tongues.

# The Power of Pentecost

(4)   By making yourself ready and available to be used by God – waiting on God, hungering and thirsting after Him!

(5)   By lifting up Jesus in your teaching of the Word of God.

(6)   By boldly moving out in faith and ministering to the needs of people as the Holy Spirit anoints, prompts, and urges you.

You need to spend time in prayer, spend time in God's presence, become sensitive to the Holy Spirit and yield yourself to Him.

Open yourself up to operate in the gifts of the Spirit and expect to be used by God.

Prepare yourself – make yourself available to God to be used by Him – open yourself up to Him.

As God anoints you, prompts you, leads you, and the unction comes, be bold to instantly obey God. Wait on God and wait for the unction to come.

You can believe God for the following things:

- To use you more in the gifts of the Spirit.
- To increase the supernatural in your ministry.
- For a greater measure of the anointing.
- For increased sensitivity to the Holy Spirit and His voice.
- For the people to place a demand on the anointing and ministry gift on your life.

God has equipped every believer with supernatural power.

The anointing of God to supernaturally destroy the works of the devil does not belong exclusively to the five-fold ministry:  Apostle, Prophet, Evangelist, Pastor, Teacher. It belongs to you as well.

*"And He Himself gave some to be apostles, some prophets, some evangelists, and some pastors and teachers for the equipping of the saints for the work of ministry, for the edifying of the body of Christ."*
                                                        **Ephesians 4:11, 12**

The purpose of the five-fold ministry gifts God set in the church is to teach and train all believers so they can go out and supernaturally minister to the world.

Those in the five-fold ministry are not to be the "star performers." Every Christian is to be a supernatural minister. We have sat on the church pews long enough like spiritual spectators doing nothing.

We have the unscriptural concept that Christians are to come to church week after week and be ministered to and prayed for by God's superstars (those in the elite five-fold ministry). That is wrong!  That is not the New Testament!

God has anointed you to supernaturally heal the sick. God has anointed you to supernaturally deliver people out of the bondage in which they are living.

The normal Christian life is a supernatural life.

So many times we have had the wrong idea that we are to come to church and see the preacher perform miracles. We look at the five-fold ministry as God's superstars, as if only they have the supernatural gifts of the Spirit and the power to heal the sick and cast out demons.

# The Power of Pentecost

God's supernatural power is for all believers in Christ.

God's healing and miracle power is for you.

The divine supernatural gifts of the Spirit are for all believers.

The gifts of the Spirit are the "Power Tools" God gives us to fulfill our ministries, carry out the great commission, and destroy the works of the devil.

Spiritual empowering equips the believer for service.

Acts 2:16-19

## HOW TO OPERATE IN THE GIFTS OF THE SPIRIT

### NUMBER 1

Get dissatisfied with being a pew warmer in the church and make up your mind to be a New Testament believer actively fulfilling the great commission and DOING the works of Jesus.

Mark 16:15-20

### NUMBER 2

Be continually filled with the Holy Spirit and be a clean, yielded, available vessel for God's anointing to flow through.

Ephesians 5:18

Remember that all ministry flows out of your relationship with the Holy Spirit.

### NUMBER 3

Earnestly desire to be used in the gifts by actively seeking God in prayer.

1 Corinthians 14:1, 12<br>Hebrews 11:6

### NUMBER 4

Increase your knowledge of spiritual gifts by studying what the Bible teaches about them.

1 Corinthians 12:1

Increased Biblical knowledge will increase your faith to operate in the gifts.

### NUMBER 5

Love people and minister to their needs with the love of God.

1 Corinthians 13:1-8<br>Galatians 5:6

*"And when Jesus went out He saw a great multitude; and He was moved with compassion for them, and healed their sick."*

Matthew 14:14

### NUMBER 6

Expect the Holy Spirit to manifest His gifts through you as you boldly step out in obedience to His leading.

Luke 11:13<br>Hebrews 2:4

# The Power of Pentecost

**Important:** Moving in the GIFTS involves a willingness to TAKE RISKS — it is not sitting back playing it SAFE! You must be willing to step out as you sense the Holy Spirit and His anointing, His promptings, His voice speaking to you. As you receive His thoughts, words, pictures or impressions, then boldly step out and walk on the water. Reject the fear of man, be willing to be a fool for Jesus for the sake of the Gospel.

*"He who believes in Me, as the Scripture has said, out of his heart will flow rivers of living water."*

John 7:38

## RECOGNIZING YOUR AUTHORITY AND ABILITY IN CHRIST

*"But you shall receive power — ability, efficiency and might — when the Holy Spirit has come upon you; and you shall be My witnesses in Jerusalem and all Judea and Samaria and to the ends — the very bounds — of the earth."*

Acts 1:8 (AMP)

This is how God sees you and what God says you can do.

(1) Your body is the temple of the Holy Spirit. The Greater One lives in you.

(2) All believers have Christ's authority and supernatural anointing to do the works of Christ on the earth.

(3) God has equipped you with supernatural power to bring deliverance to suffering humanity.

(4) All believers are filled with Christ's fullness.

(5) God has given you the supernatural gifts of the Spirit to destroy the works of the devil.

### KEY TRUTH:

**Every believer in Christ should have five supernatural signs following them as they reach out to a needy world.**

*"And these signs will follow those who believe: In My Name they will cast out demons; they will speak with new tongues; they will take up serpents; and if they drink anything deadly, it will by no means hurt them; they will lay hands on the sick, and they will recover."*

Mark 16:17, 18

### FIVE SUPERNATURAL SIGNS

**NUMBER 1**     As a New Testament Christian, you cast out demons in the name of the Lord Jesus Christ.

# The Power of Pentecost

__NUMBER 2__     As a New Testament Christian, you speak with other tongues.

__NUMBER 3__     As a New Testament Christian, you enforce Satan's defeat and destroy the works of the devil.

__NUMBER 4__     As a New Testament Christian, you walk and live in divine protection.

__NUMBER 5__     As a New Testament Christian, you lay hands on the sick and they will be healed.

These are the five supernatural signs that Jesus said should follow you — not just those in full-time ministry or leaders in the church.

## HOW TO STAY FILLED WITH THE SPIRIT

*"And do not be drunk with wine, in which is dissipation; but be filled with the Spirit."*

**Ephesians 5:18**

God the Holy Spirit is a person who wants to completely control your life so that the Lord Jesus Christ may be made real to you and then through you, to others.

Without His control you will be a powerless, ineffective Christian.

(1)  Surrender your will totally to God.

*"...the Holy Spirit whom God has given to those who obey him."*

**Acts 5:32**

(2)  Be thorough in confession and repentance of all known sin.

*"He who covers his sins will not prosper, But whoever confesses and forsakes them will have mercy."*

**Proverbs 28:13**

*"Nevertheless the solid foundation of God stands, having this seal: 'The Lord knows those who are His,' and, 'Let everyone who names the name of Christ depart from iniquity.'"*

**2 Timothy 2:19**

(3)  Ask God to fill you afresh with His Spirit.

*"If you, then, being evil, know how to give good gifts to your children, how much more will your heavenly Father give the Holy Spirit to those who ask Him."*

**Luke 11:13**

(4)  Believe that He will and thank Him for doing so.

*"Whatsoever is not of faith is sin."*     **Romans 14:23 (KJV)**

# The Power of Pentecost

Allow the Holy Spirit to manifest Himself in whichever way He chooses by being obedient to His promptings.

These conditions need to be fulfilled constantly in order to maintain the Spirit-filled life.

(5) Pray in tongues consistently to charge and build up your inward man and feed your spirit on the Word of God.

*"But you, beloved, building yourselves up on your most holy faith, praying in the Holy Spirit."*

Jude 20

*"But He answered and said, 'It is written, Man shall not live by bread alone, but by every word that proceeds from the mouth of God.'"*

Matthew 4:4

# LESSON: 2     Understanding The Anointing

**KEY VERSE:** Luke 4:18

*"The Spirit of the Lord is upon Me, Because He has anointed Me to preach the gospel to the poor; He has sent Me to heal the broken-hearted, To proclaim liberty to the captives And recovery of sight to the blind, To set at liberty those who are oppressed..."*

**KEY TRUTH:** Our ministries must operate in the anointing of the Holy Spirit, otherwise all we have is DEAD RELIGION.

## THE ANOINTED WORD

*"It is the Spirit who gives life; the flesh profits nothing. The words that I speak to you are spirit, and they are life."*

John 6:63

*"For the word of God is living and powerful, and sharper than any two-edged sword, piercing even to the division of soul and spirit, and of joints and marrow, and is a discerner of the thoughts and intents of the heart."*

Hebrews 4:12

*"For our gospel did not come to you in word only, but also in power, and in the Holy Spirit..."*

1 Thessalonians 1:5

*"And they went out and preached everywhere, the Lord working with them and confirming the word through the accompanying signs. Amen."*

Mark 16:20

- The anointing will accompany the preaching and the teaching of God's Word.
- The anointing is on the Word.
- God's power is in His Word.

*"For I am not ashamed of the gospel of Christ, for it is the power of God to salvation for everyone who believes..."*

Romans 1:16

- The anointing of God is transmitted through the preaching of the Gospel of Christ.

**There is an anointing:**

| | |
|---|---|
| to pray for the sick | to give altar calls |
| to cast out demons | to win the lost to Jesus |
| to present the Gospel of Christ | to teach the Bible with revelation knowledge |

# Understanding The Anointing

**PERSONAL NOTES**

*"And my speech and my preaching were not with persuasive words of human wisdom, but in demonstration of the Spirit and of power, that your faith should not be in the wisdom of men but in the power of God."*

1 Corinthians 2:4, 5

Paul was anointed to preach and demonstrate the Gospel.

## WHAT IS THE ANOINTING?

The anointing is not human strength or fleshly ability.

The anointing is the presence and power of God manifest.

The anointing is the spiritual equipment to get the job done – it is God's tools to get the job done.

The anointing is the supernatural ability God gives to you to flow and function in your area of ministry.

**There is an anointing:**

| | |
|---|---|
| to prophesy | to preach the Gospel |
| to teach God's Word | to cast out demons |
| to heal the sick | to operate in spiritual gifts |

The anointing is a TANGIBLE, SUPERNATURAL SUBSTANCE. It is the power of God in manifestation.

*"Indeed it came to pass, when the trumpeters and singers were as one, to make one sound to be heard in praising and thanking the Lord, and when they lifted up their voice with the trumpets and cymbals and instruments of music, and praised the Lord, saying:*
*'For He is good, For His mercy endures forever.'*
*that the house, the house of the Lord, was filled with a cloud,*
*so that the priests could not continue ministering because of the cloud; for the glory of the Lord filled the house of God."*

2 Chronicles 5:13, 14

The power of God and the anointing of God was so strong in manifestation in the Old Testament worship services, that everybody fell out under the power. They could not stand up because of the glory of God.

The anointing is a manifestation of the Holy Spirit where the Holy Spirit moves in the natural realm, and we can contact Him with our senses.

The anointing of God is tangible, it is real, and you can feel the power of God. It is like a warm glow, like electricity flowing through your being.

When I am ministering in the Spirit and laying hands on people, I often feel a charge of electricity coming from my stomach area, rising up to my chest, and flowing down through my arms and into the people.

# Understanding The Anointing

The anointing is the Holy Spirit in action where He moves out into the sense realm.

The anointing of God is the manifestation of the power of God.

You can't buy the anointing like Simon the Sorcerer tried to do in the Book of Acts.

**With the call of God comes the anointing to fulfill your call.**

To get the anointing on the scene, just begin to share the Word of God and lift up Jesus.

## POWER AND ANOINTING

*"Behold, I give you the authority to trample on serpents and scorpions, and over all the power of the enemy, and nothing shall by any means hurt you."*
Luke 10:19

*"The Spirit of the Lord is upon Me, because He has anointed Me To preach the gospel to the poor; He has sent Me to heal the brokenhearted, To proclaim liberty to the captives and recovery of sight to the blind, To set at liberty those who are oppressed; To proclaim the acceptable year of the Lord."*
Luke 4:18

**"Power"** means force, strength, might, ability, and dominion over all.

**"Anointing"** means:

   (1) to smear, to run on, to pour all over with oil (Psalm 133).
   (2) to furnish what is needed to get the job done – Divine equipment.

When God calls you, He anoints you and equips you with His ability.

The anointing of God is the supernatural energy of God. It is the divine enablement of God.

The Bible says about Jesus in Luke 4:18 that He was:

   • ANOINTED TO PREACH
   • ANOINTED TO HEAL
   • ANOINTED TO BRING DELIVERANCE

In other words, it must be the Spirit of God who anoints you TO DO something. You see, there are separate anointings involved.

*"How God anointed Jesus of Nazareth with the Holy Spirit and with power, who went about doing good and healing all who were oppressed by the devil, for God was with him."*

Acts 10:38

Jesus was anointed with the Holy Spirit and power. He was given a POWER ANOINTING to heal the sick.

# Understanding The Anointing

© 1994 The Believer's School of Training, Rev. Norman K. Robertson

*"You have loved righteousness and hated lawlessness; Therefore God, Your God, has anointed You with the oil of gladness more than your companions."*

**Hebrews 1:9**

Jesus was anointed (to smear on and cover in) with the oil of gladness anointing.

So there are definite, separate anointings – various anointings for specific people.

## THREE ANOINTINGS

*"Let your garments always be white, And let your head lack no oil."*

**Ecclesiastes 9:8**

In Old Testament times men were set apart, consecrated to the office of ministry by the anointing with oil.

The anointing oil was a type of the Holy Spirit's anointing.

**(1)  The anointing of the Prophet's Office.**

**1 Kings 19:15, 16**
**Psalm 105:15**
**Luke 4:18**

Jesus was anointed by the Spirit, not only for the prophet's office, but for all five-fold ministry offices.

**(2)  They were anointed in the Old Testament to the Priestly Office.**
**Exodus 29:4-7**
**Exodus 30:30**

**(3)  Then there was the anointing to the King's Office.**

**1 Samuel 16:12, 13**

1 Samuel 16:1 gives us sound instructions for supernaturally effective ministry – *"...Fill your horn with oil, and go..."*

Not every believer in the Old Testament had the anointing.

Three Old Testament anointings:

- **Prophet's Anointing**
- **Priest's Anointing**
- **King's Anointing**

The anointing is a manifestation of the power of God – you can sense it and feel it in the physical realm.

The anointing of God is the Holy Spirit ACTING, REVEALING, and MANIFESTING in the natural realm.

The anointing of God is TRANSFERABLE. It is tangible and it can be picked up and transferred from one believer to the next.

# Understanding The Anointing

- All the Miracles of the Old Testament
- All the Miracles in the Ministry of Elijah and Elisha
- All the Miracles in the Ministry of Jesus
- All the Miracles in the New Testament Church – **were released and produced because of the anointing of God!**

Think about Moses, Joshua, Samson, Elijah, Elisha, Daniel, the Lord Jesus Christ, the Apostle Paul, Peter, and believers in the New Testament Church.

Think about the impact of their ministries and the supernatural miracles, healings, and deliverances that took place because of the anointing on their lives.

## LEADERS ANOINTED IN BIBLE DAYS

The Anointing was upon:

| | | | |
|---|---|---|---|
| **JOSEPH** | Genesis 41:38 | **MOSES** | Numbers 11:17 |
| **JOSHUA** | Numbers 27:18 | **OTHNIEL** | Judges 3:10 |
| **SAMSON** | Judges 14:6 | **SAUL** | 1 Samuel 10:10 |
| **DAVID** | 1 Samuel 16:13; Psalm 89:20 | **JESUS** | Luke 4:18; Acts 10:38 |
| **DANIEL** | Daniel 6:3 | **PAUL** | Acts 19:11, 12 |

## THE ANOINTING UPON ELIJAH AND ELISHA

Elijah was anointed of God and moved in the miracle power of God.

| | |
|---|---|
| **1 Kings 17:1** | • Proclaims a drought for three and one-half years |
| **1 Kings 17:2-6** | • Supernaturally fed and sustained by ravens |
| **1 Kings 17:8-16** | • Miraculous multiplication of the widow's oil and flour |
| **1 Kings 17:17-22** | • Raises from the dead the son of the widow woman |
| **1 Kings 18:17-40** | • Challenges 450 Prophets of Baal and calls fire down from Heaven |
| **1 Kings 18:41-45** | • After three and one-half years, ends the drought |
| **1 Kings 18:46** | • With supernatural speed, outruns the chariots of Ahab for twenty miles |
| **2 Kings 2:8, 9** | • Splits the River Jordan |

**Elisha asked for a Double Portion of the Anointing on Elijah.**

Elijah's anointing was transferred to Elisha.

**2 Kings 2:9, 13, 14**

## THE MIRACLE MINISTRY OF ELISHA

| | |
|---|---|
| **2 Kings 2:19-22** | • Miracle healing of the polluted water and barren land |

# Understanding The Anointing

**PERSONAL NOTES**

| | |
|---|---|
| 2 Kings 2:23, 24 | • Curses the youths who mocked him |
| 2 Kings 3:15-18 | • Miracle of the irrigation canals |
| 2 Kings 4:1-7 | • Miracle multiplication of the oil for the widow and her son to pay off all debts |
| 2 Kings 4:8-37 | • Elisha raises the Shunnamite woman's son from the dead. |
| 2 Kings 5:1-14 | • Naaman is cleansed of leprosy. |
| 2 Kings 6:4-7 | • The miracle of the floating axe head. |
| 2 Kings 13:20, 21 | • Elisha's dead bones were reservoirs of God's anointing and caused a dead man to live. |

## THE ANOINTING IN THE LIFE OF JESUS

Study the anointing on the life and ministry of Jesus. Did you know that over sixty percent of the ministry of Jesus was healing the sick and casting out demons? That makes it important!

*"How God anointed Jesus of Nazareth with the Holy Spirit and with power, who went about doing good and healing all who were oppressed by the devil, for God was with Him."*

**Acts 10:38**

Jesus said, "I came to do the will of my Father."

He said, "The words I speak are my Father's words."

He said, "I and my Father are one."

He said, "If you have seen me, then you have seen the Father."

He said, "The works that I do are my Father's works."

**Luke 4:14-19**

The anointing is for action.

The anointing always brings blessing, it always brings healing and deliverance.

The anointing is tangible. It can be felt.

**Mark 5:29, 30**

## RESULTS OF THE ANOINTING IN JESUS' MINISTRY

| | |
|---|---|
| Matthew 4:23, 24 | · Healing all sickness, all disease, and all sick people |
| Matthew 8:1-4 | · The leper is cleansed |
| Matthew 8:5-13 | · The Centurion's servant is healed of palsy and delivered from demonic torment |
| Matthew 8:14, 15 | · Peter's mother-in-law healed of fever |
| Matthew 8:16, 17 | · Devils cast out and the whole town healed |
| Matthew 8:23-27 | · Calms the tempest by rebuking the wind and the sea |
| Matthew 8:28-34 | · Two demon-possessed men set free |

# Understanding The Anointing

| | | |
|---|---|---|
| **Matthew 9:2-8** | · | Healed the paralytic man |
| **Matthew 9:18-26** | · | Jairus' daughter raised up from the dead, and the woman with the issue of blood cured |
| **Matthew 9:27-31** | · | Two blind men healed and sight restored |
| **Matthew 9:32, 33** | · | A demon-possessed man is delivered |
| **Matthew 9:35** | · | Jesus heals every sickness and every disease among the people |
| **Matthew 12:9-13** | · | Jesus heals the man with the withered hand |
| **Matthew 12:15** | · | Jesus heals great multitudes |
| **Matthew 12:22** | · | Jesus heals and delivers a demon-possessed dumb and blind man |
| **Matthew 14:14** | · | The compassion of Jesus heals crowds of sick people |
| **Matthew 14:35, 36** | · | Jesus heals all who were sick in Gennesaret |
| **Matthew 15:22-28** | · | Woman of Canaan's daughter is delivered from demons and made whole |
| **Matthew 15:30, 31** | · | Crowds of blind, maimed, lame, and mute – Jesus makes them whole |
| **Matthew 17:14-21** | · | Jesus heals and delivers the epileptic boy |
| **Matthew 19:2** | · | He heals great multitudes |
| **Matthew 20:29-34** | · | Jesus restores sight to two blind men at Jericho |
| **Matthew 21:14** | · | Jesus heals the blind and the lame in the temple |

*"The blind see and the lame walk; the lepers are cleansed and the deaf hear; the dead are raised up and the poor have the gospel preached to them."*
                                        Matthew 11:5

*"Men of Israel, hear these words: Jesus of Nazareth, a Man attested by God to you by miracles, wonders, and signs which God did through Him in your midst, as you yourselves also know..."*
                                        Acts 2:22

*"But Jesus said, 'Somebody touched Me, for I perceived power going out from Me.'"*
                                        Luke 8:46

We see here that Jesus was a carrier or a vehicle of God's anointing.

Jesus carried God's divine power in Him and it flowed out from Him.

Where did Jesus get His anointing from?

*"How God anointed Jesus of Nazareth with the Holy Spirit and with power, who went about doing good and healing all who were oppressed by the devil, for God was with Him."*
                                        Acts 10:38

# Understanding The Anointing

**PERSONAL NOTES**

(1) Jesus was not anointed because He was the Son of God.

(2) Jesus was anointed because God WAS WITH HIM.

When God is with you, He anoints you — so then any New Testament believer can become a vehicle, a carrier of the same anointing and the same power with which Jesus walked.

WHEN GOD IS WITH YOU, then His anointing and His power are with you.

*"...Because He has anointed Me"*                    Luke 4:18

Jesus was anointed:

   (1)  to preach

   (2)  to heal

   (3)  to minister deliverance

   (4)  to open blind eyes

   (5)  to set free the oppressed

*"As You sent Me into the world, I also have sent them into the world."*

John 17:18

Here Jesus is praying to the Father for all New Testament believers, "As you sent me — I am sending them."

John 17:20-22

How was Jesus sent? How was Jesus equipped?

***"How God anointed Jesus of Nazareth with the Holy Spirit and with power, who went about doing good and healing all who were oppressed by the devil, for God was with Him."***

Acts 10:38

So Jesus put the same anointing on His disciples that the Father had put on Him.

Jesus was a vehicle, a carrier, a conductor of God's power and anointing.

New Testament disciples — all of us — have been given and are equipped as vehicles of the same anointing Jesus had.

John 17:18

John 17:22

God was with Jesus and God is with us.

Acts 10:38

Matthew 28:20

The anointing, the virtue, and the power that was inside Jesus, is **now in us** as believers. **You** are a vehicle of God's anointing.

***"And my speech and my preaching were not with persuasive words of human wisdom, but in demonstration of the Spirit and of power. That your faith should not be in the wisdom of men but in the power of God.***

1 Corinthians 2:4, 5

# Understanding The Anointing

*"For the kingdom of God is not in word but in power."*

1 Corinthians 4:20

What is the purpose of God demonstrating His power and anointing with miracles, signs, and wonders?

The reason why the power of God should be in demonstration is because local churches and services where miracles, healings, signs, and wonders are not happening are opposite to the New Testament pattern for the church. There is a quality of God's Spirit lacking in those churches. The anointing is missing.

Manifestations of God's power and public demonstration of God's healing anointing is essential in the church today because it gives real evidence that Jesus Christ is alive. **CHRISTIANITY is not only a message but also a ministry – a miracle ministry.**

*"And with great power the apostles gave witness to the resurrection of the Lord Jesus. And great grace was upon them all."*

Acts 4:33

God's purpose in manifesting His power and anointing:

    is not to exalt men

    is not to build the name of your ministry or church

    is not to magnify any individual

But, it is always to exalt Jesus and to set people free.

Acts 4:33

(1) GREAT POWER – it is always the will of God that His power be manifested in healings and miracles.

(2) WITNESS – the anointing is always to give evidence and bear witness that the Bible Jesus is ALIVE.

(3) GREAT GRACE – was upon the New Testament believers. Grace is the divine enablement to do the work of God.

## DEMONSTRATIONS OF THE ANOINTING IN THE BOOK OF ACTS CHURCH

(1) Peter's power preaching on the day of Pentecost caused 3,000 people to be born again and follow Christ.

Acts 2:41

(2) The miracle healing of the crippled beggar at the gate of the temple, through the name of Jesus.

Acts 3:1-16

# Understanding The Anointing

© 1994 The Believer's School of Training, Rev. Norman K. Robertson

**PERSONAL NOTES**

The anointing of God is released though the name of Jesus.

**Acts 4:7-10**

(3) The mass healing of the multitudes in the streets of Jerusalem, through the SHADOW of Peter and the hands of the Apostles.

**Acts 5:12, 15, 16**

(4) Stephen was empowered by the anointing of the Holy Spirit to manifest "great" wonders and signs among the people.

**Acts 6:8, 10**

(5) Philip, a deacon, preaches Christ in Samaria to the multitudes with supernatural signs following the preaching. The results were MASS SALVATIONS, MASS HEALINGS, MASS DELIVERANCES, bringing joy to the whole city! The anointing of God affected the whole city.

**Acts 8:5-8, 12**

(6) Philip was supernaturally "translated" – transported twenty-five miles from the desert to the city of Azotus after leading the Ethiopian Eunuch to Christ.

**Acts 8:39, 40**

(7) The Holy Spirit fell upon and baptized Cornelius and his whole household in Acts 10.

**Acts 10:44-46**

(8) Paul, preaching the Gospel at Lystra, ministers divine healing to a cripple who had never walked.

**Acts 14:8-11**

(9) Signs and wonders were manifested through the anointing upon Paul and Barnabas.

**Acts 15:12**

(10) In Philippi, Paul casts the demon spirit of divination (fortune-telling) out of a young woman.

**Acts 16:16-18**

(11) Special miracles through anointed prayer cloths.    **Acts 19:11, 12**

(12) In Acts 20:7-12, Paul preached a long sermon. At midnight, a young man called Eutychus fell out the window from the third floor onto the pavement and was dead. Paul stopped the service, went down, and raised him up from the dead. A supernatural miracle anointing brought new life into a dead man.

## SUPERNATURAL POWER FOR BELIEVERS TODAY

Luke 24:49    •    **Power** from on High (Heaven)
Acts 1:8    •    **Power** (DUNAMIS POWER)

# Understanding The Anointing

Acts 4:33          •          **Power** to be a witness

The power of God in our lives is to give evidence of the reality of the resurrection of Jesus Christ – that Jesus is alive.                         Acts 4:33

The anointing of God bears witness that Jesus is alive.

The anointing of God is to reveal to the lost that Jesus the SAVIOR, HEALER, and DELIVERER lives today.

> 1 Corinthians 2:4, 5
> 1 Corinthians 4:20
> Mark 16:20
> 1 Thessalonians 1:5

If there is not a demonstration of the Spirit and power – then it is not the Gospel.

Signs following the Gospel witness to the reality of the resurrection of Jesus and set people free.

## POWER = "DUNAMIS" =
(1) **Explosive power (DYNAMITE)**
(2) **Miracle energy**
(3) **Divine ability**
(4) **Mighty works**
(5) **Power in action in performing miracles**

*"As You sent Me into the world, I also have sent them into the world."*
                         John 17:18

**QUESTION:**   How was Jesus sent?
**ANSWER:**    Acts 10:38

Jesus has equipped us with the same anointing that He was equipped with.

*"Most assuredly, I say to you, he who believes in Me, the works that I do he will do also; and greater works than these he will do, because I go to My Father."*
                         John 14:12

It is very clear from studying the New Testament and especially the Book of Acts, that it is God's plan and God's will for Christians today to walk in His anointing and operate in Holy Spirit power!

## GOD'S PLAN FOR NEW TESTAMENT CHRISTIANS
As New Testament believers we are told:

**NUMBER 1**   To be full of and controlled by the Holy Spirit.
                         Acts 4:8 (AMP)

# Understanding The Anointing

**PERSONAL NOTES**

<u>NUMBER 2</u>    To speak in tongues and have rivers of living water flowing out of our inner man.

> Acts 2:4
> John 7:38

<u>NUMBER 3</u>    To have the power of God to do all things, where nothing shall be impossible.

> Mark 9:23

<u>NUMBER 4</u>    To cast out demons.      Mark 16:17

<u>NUMBER 5</u>    To heal the sick of all kinds of disease.    Luke 9:1, 2

<u>NUMBER 6</u>    To cleanse the lepers and incurable diseases.

> Matthew 10:8

<u>NUMBER 7</u>    To raise the dead.      John 11:40, 43, 44

<u>NUMBER 8</u>    To get all prayers answered.      John 15:7

<u>NUMBER 9</u>    To exercise power over all the power of the devil and destroy the works of the devil.

> Luke 10:19
> James 4:7

<u>NUMBER 10</u>    To do works as great and even greater than Jesus did.

> John 14:12
> Matthew 11:2-5

<u>NUMBER 11</u>    To proclaim the good news to the poor.    Luke 4:18

<u>NUMBER 12</u>    To set the captives free by the anointing of God.

> Mark 6:13

<u>NUMBER 13</u>    To restore sight to the blind.      Luke 7:21

<u>NUMBER 14</u>    To restore hearing to the deaf.      Matthew 11:5

<u>NUMBER 15</u>    To cause cripples to walk and the lame to be made whole.

> Acts 14:8-10

# Understanding The Anointing

**NUMBER 16**    To be immune from poisons and live in divine protection, where nothing of the enemy can harm or destroy us.

**Mark 16:18**

**NUMBER 17**    To execute judgement upon God's enemies by the power of the Holy Spirit.

**Acts 5:3-10**

**NUMBER 18**    To impart the baptism of the Holy Spirit to other believers.

**Acts 8:17**

**NUMBER 19**    To exercise all nine gifts of the Spirit.    **1 Corinthians 12:7-11**

**NUMBER 20**    To impart spiritual gifts to other believers.  **Romans 1:11**

**NUMBER 21**    To bind and loose and exercise authority, in the name of Jesus, over all the works of the devil.

**Matthew 18:18**

**NUMBER 22**    To receive supernatural guidance, instruction, and direction from the Holy Spirit.

**Acts 13:2**

**NUMBER 23**    To carry the presence and anointing of God and manifest all kinds of miracles, signs, and wonders.

**Hebrews 2:4**

**NUMBER 24**    To walk in complete freedom from the bondage of sickness, poverty, false doctrines, and demon powers.

**Galatians 5:1**

**NUMBER 25**    To preach the uncompromised Word of God with power and boldness.

**Acts 4:31**

## THE ANOINTING WITHIN

*"But you have an anointing from the Holy One, and you know all things."*

**1 John 2:20**

*"But the anointing which you have received from Him abides in you, and you do not need that anyone teach you; but as the same anointing teaches you concerning all things, and is true, and is not a lie, and just as it has taught you, you will abide in Him."*

**1 John 2:27**

# Understanding The Anointing

© 1994 The Believer's School of Training, Rev. Norman K. Robertson

**PERSONAL NOTES**

Every New Testament believer has an anointing to be taught by the Holy Spirit and guided by Him.

John 14:26
John 16:13

Because we are born again and Spirit filled, we all have an anointing in us. The anointing within enables us:

* To be TAUGHT by the Great Teacher, the Holy Spirit.    John 14:26

* To be GUIDED and DIRECTED by the Holy Spirit.    John 16:13

* To WALK in DIVINE LOVE.    Romans 5:5

* To WORSHIP by the Spirit.    Philippians 3:3

* To PRAY supernaturally.    Romans 8:26, 27

* To live a SANCTIFIED LIFE.    1 Peter 1:2

*"Let your garments always be white, And let your head lack no oil."*

Ecclesiastes 9:8

*"But my horn you have exalted like a wild ox; I have been anointed with fresh oil."*

Psalm 92:10

Literal Hebrew translation states:

*"My horn (means My Strength) you have exalted like a wild ox because I have been anointed with fresh oil."*

**Note:** The source of our strength is the anointing.

## THE NEED FOR FRESH OIL

What happens when you hit a SLUMP in your Christian life or in your ministry? You are still living for God, still praying, still reading your Bible, still singing in the church band, still preaching on Sundays, etc.

BUT ...

It has become a drag, a drudgery. You feel dry, flat. You've lost your cutting edge. You are stale. It's dull, boring, and hard work.

WHY? WHAT IS IT? WHAT'S WRONG?

It's a lack of FRESH OIL.

What you need is fresh oil, a fresh anointing.

There is a desperate need today for the anointing — you need fresh oil and anointing from Heaven to accomplish the purposes of God.

# Understanding The Anointing

While there may be one initial baptism in the Holy Spirit – one initial overwhelming experience – There are hundreds of fresh infillings and refillings of the Holy Spirit available for every believer. Read the Book of Acts.

*"And they were all filled with the Holy Spirit and began to speak with other tongues, as the Spirit gave them utterance."*

Acts 2:4

*"And when they had prayed, the place where they were assembled together was shaken; and they were all filled with the Holy Spirit, and they spoke the word of God with boldness."*

Acts 4:31

*"And do not be drunk with wine, in which is dissipation; but be filled with the Spirit."*

Ephesians 5:18

*"...I have been anointed with fresh oil."*        Psalm 92:10

You must have the life, the power, the anointing, the river, and the oil of God in your PRESENT experience. The anointing is the life of Jesus on you and flowing through you!

You must receive a fresh anointing of the Holy Spirit every day.

Psalm 92:10

Ephesians 5:18

What you had in 1974 will not help you today. The oil of 1974 is used up, dried up, drained, and won't help you.

## HOW TO RECEIVE A FRESH TOUCH FROM GOD DAILY

(1) A consistent prayer life and daily communion with God – spiritual hunger.

Isaiah 44:3

Hosea 10:11, 12

Jude 20

(2) Living a lifestyle of purity and holiness.        Ecclesiastes 9:8

(3) Spending time reading, studying, and meditating in the Word of God.

Hebrews 4:12

(4) Being a fervent worshiper.        John 4:24

# Understanding The Anointing

**PERSONAL NOTES**

(5) Being committed to walking in God's love. The love of God releases the power of God.

Galatians 5:6

(6) Taking your place in active service for God and ministering to the needs of people around you.

Luke 4:18

*"Dead flies putrefy the perfumer's ointment, And cause it to give off a foul odor..."*

Ecclesiastes 10:1

"Dead flies" or "flies of death" means:

* Ministry of death
* Dead preaching
* Dead religion
* No works of God manifested

The anointing can wane, decrease, diminish, or become stagnant in our lives. We need fresh oil or we can stink spiritually and operate in dead works.

By being filled with the Spirit you will have a fresh anointing every day.

*"And do not be drunk with wine, in which is dissipation; but be filled with the Spirit, speaking to one another in psalms and hymns and spiritual songs, singing and making melody in your heart to the Lord, giving thanks always for all things to God the Father in the name of our Lord Jesus Christ, submitting to one another in the fear of God."*

Ephesians 5:18-21

Six results of being filled afresh:

(1) Speaking Psalms (spiritual poems)

(2) Singing spiritual songs

(3) Full of joy

(4) Full of thanksgiving to God

(5) Walking in the fear of God (in submission to each other)

(6) A bold testimony (Acts 4:31, 33)

**IMPORTANT:** *Take time this week to review the powerful truths and Scriptures in these two lessons and visualize how God wants you to walk in the supernatural realm of the Holy Spirit.*

# Response To Truth
## *Lessons 1 and 2*

**PERSONAL NOTES**

## KEY QUESTIONS:

(1) Why is the anointing so essential?

(2) What are the five things we can do to stay filled with the Holy Spirit?

(3) List ten significant events of the Holy Spirit's outpouring in the 20th century?

(4) Explain the three anointings of the Old Testament.

(5) How was Jesus anointed and what were the results?

## MEMORY WORK

1 Thessalonians 1:5

Romans 1:16

Acts 4:33

## PERSONAL APPLICATION

(1) Are you currently filled with the Holy Spirit or are you trying to get by on last year's anointing?

(2) Write out the Six-Fold Holy Spirit End Time Prophecy in Acts 2:17-19 and see how it applies to your life and ministry.

(3) How many of the five supernatural signs of Mark 16:17,18 operate in your life?

(4) When you share the Gospel with someone in need do you expect the Holy Spirit to back up what you say with signs following?

(5) Have you experienced the touch of God's anointing upon your life? If not, are you HUNGRY and THIRSTY for God and His anointing?

## RECOMMENDED READING

Dr. Yonggi Cho, *The Holy Spirit, My Senior Partner*

Norvel Hayes, *Endued With Power*

# LESSON: 3 | Keys To The Anointing

**PERSONAL NOTES**

**KEY VERSE:** Psalm 92:10 *"But my horn You have exalted like a wild ox; I have been anointed with fresh oil."*

**KEY TRUTH:** We cannot live on past revivals and the past anointings we experienced. We must be people who are anointed of God and walk in a fresh anointing daily.

## WHAT IS THE ANOINTING?

You know what it isn't. You should be able to discern between the **anointed** and the **unanointed.**

The anointing is the hand of God, the power and life force of God upon your ministry. The anointing is God flowing through you.

Without the anointing, you are empty, with nothing to give people and there will be no results. Religious programs and HYPE are not the anointing.

Anointing means the touch of God upon our lives.

*"But you have an anointing from the Holy One, and you know all things...But the anointing which you have received from Him abides in you, and you do not need that anyone should teach you; but as the same anointing teaches you concerning all things, and is true, and is not a lie, and just as it has taught you, you will abide in Him."*

1 John 2:20, 27

**NOTICE:** It's the anointing that TEACHES AND COMMUNICATES LIFE to people and not Biblical knowledge or the memorization of facts.
Being loaded with information doesn't teach. It's THE ANOINTING that teaches and produces life.

Let the anointing of God carry you and don't try working for God in the flesh. Be a river, not a stagnant swamp.

The anointing cannot be **worked up, pumped up, or hyped up**. You get it by spending time with God. You must have communion with God. He is the Anointer and the Power Source.

As the Lord calls you into a specific office of ministry; He gives you an anointing to stand in that office.

There is a specific anointing that goes with your calling.

If God has not anointed you to do something, don't attempt to function in that office or ministry because nothing will happen and there will be no results.

Only the Holy Spirit can anoint you, call you, and supernaturally equip you. Man cannot impart it to you. **It's the anointing that changes you into another man when you minister.**

# Keys To The Anointing

**PERSONAL NOTES**

*"Then the Spirit of the Lord will come upon you, and you will prophesy with them and be turned into another man."*

1 Samuel 10:6

**Exodus 30:31-33** warns us not to substitute anything for the anointing – not man's ability, not human personality, not hype, not religious activities.

The presence of the Lord is the anointing.

The characteristic feature of Jesus' presence and the anointing is not tongues or prophecy, it is LIFE!

When you are anointed to speak or to teach, the power of God is behind your words. God's life is backing what you say, and your words do not fall to the ground empty.

Our anointing must be fresh and up to date. We must never lose the anointing.

## UNDERSTANDING THE ANOINTING

*"But you have an anointing from the Holy One, and you know all things."*

1 John 2:20

SAY:  "I have an anointing."

*"But the anointing which you have received from Him abides in you, and you do not need that anyone teach you; but as the same anointing teaches you concerning all things, and is true, and is not a lie, and just as it has taught you, you will abide in Him.*

1 John 2:27

SAY: "The anointing abides in me."

SAY:  "The anointing abiding in me teaches me and protects me from error."

The anointing is the manifestation of God's power, God's ability, and God's presence that produces supernatural results.

You cannot live in victory without the anointing.

## WHAT IS THE PURPOSE OF THE ANOINTING?

(1)  THE ANOINTING OF GOD DESTROYS THE YOKE OF BONDAGE.

Isaiah 10:27

The purpose of the anointing is to destroy the works of the devil.

*"It shall come to pass in that day that his burden will be taken away from your shoulder, and his yoke from your neck, And the yoke will be destroyed because of the anointing oil."*

Isaiah 10:27

The anointing DESTROYS every yoke of bondage.

# Keys To The Anointing

© 1994 The Believer's School of Training, Rev. Norman K. Robertson

*"...For this purpose the Son of God was manifested, that he might destroy the works of the devil."*

1 John 3:8

The anointing doesn't break the yoke.

The anointing DESTROYS the yoke.

**"Destroy"** means pull down, tear down, demolish, shatter, eliminate, wipe out, lay in ruins.

A yoke is a heavy weight or burden.

A yoke is anything that binds or holds you in bondage.

**Yokes of Bondage = the works of the devil.**

Yokes can come in the form of sickness, sin, fear, depression, suicide, bad habits (smoking, drugs, alcohol dependency, compulsive desires and addictions) demonic influence and oppression, pornography, prostitution, the occult, homosexuality, rebellion, violence, etc.

1 John 3:8

Luke 4:18

The anointing heals, saves, sets the captives free, and delivers mankind.

**(2) THE ANOINTING OF GOD WITHIN US TEACHES ALL THINGS.**

John 16:13

We can live free from deception, error, and false teachers, because the anointing protects us and warns us within.

1 John 2:27

**(3) THE ANOINTING EQUIPS US WITH THE MIRACLE POWER OF GOD TO DO THE WORKS OF JESUS.**

John 14:12

Acts 10:38

John 17:18, 22

John 20:21

**(4) THE ANOINTING IS GIVEN TO MAKE US DYNAMIC SOULWINNERS AND BOLD WITNESSES OF THE RESURRECTION OF JESUS.**

Acts 1:8

Acts 4:31, 33

You need the anointing of God to minister to people's needs.

The anointing will cause us to walk in boldness.

# Keys To The Anointing

**PERSONAL NOTES**

*"Now when they saw the boldness of Peter and John, and perceived that they were uneducated and untrained men, they marveled. And they realized that they had been with Jesus."*

Acts 4:13

We need to be "bold", fearless people of God in these last days.

*"The wicked flee when no one pursues, But the righteous are bold as a lion."*

Proverbs 28:1

The anointing will make you a bold, radical Christian!

His ability becomes your ability.

Because of the anointing, God's ability becomes your ability.

**Example: Charles G. Finney** would walk into a factory and every single person in the building would fall out under the power of God and cry out to God for salvation.

*"For I am not ashamed of the gospel of Christ, for it is the power of God to salvation for everyone who believes..."*

Romans 1:16

The Word of God is a vital link to the anointing.

The Word of God releases the power of God.

## THE GOSPEL OF CHRIST, THE GOOD NEWS, THE WORD OF GOD, IS THE POWER OF GOD!

If we are going to walk in the power of God and experience the anointing of God, then we are going to have to study, know, live by, practice, and preach the WORD OF GOD without any compromise!

*"It is the Spirit that gives life — He is the Life-giver; the flesh conveys no benefit whatever — there is no profit in it. The words* (truths) *that I have been speaking to you are spirit and life."*

John 6:63 (AMP)

*"And they went out and preached everywhere, the Lord working with them and confirming the word through the accompanying signs. Amen."*

Mark 16:20

## HOW TO KNOW GOD'S ANOINTING

- Surrender absolutely to the Lordship of Jesus Christ.
- Believe the Word of God and what it teaches about God's anointing.
- Repent from all sin: especially unbelief, doubt, fear, things of the occult, unforgiveness, blockage of mind, wrong doctrine and the traditions of men.

# Keys To The Anointing

**PERSONAL NOTES**

- Be baptized with the Holy Spirit according to Acts 2:4.
- Read again the Scriptures in 1 John 2:20 and 2:27, which confirm that we have an anointing from the Holy One.
- By faith receive the fresh oil of the Holy Spirit according to Psalm 92:10.
- Daily hunger and thirst for the presence of God and His touch upon your life and ministry.

Isaiah 44:3

Zechariah 10:1

Don't get spiritually slack and satisfied.

**Smith Wigglesworth said**, "The only time I'm satisfied is when I'm dissatisfied!"

## DIFFERENT KINDS OF ANOINTING

Under the Old Covenant, God only anointed three kinds of people. He anointed the Prophet, the Priest, and the King. However, in the New Covenant, in the Dispensation of Grace, every child of God is ANOINTED, and today we are Priests and Kings through the Blood of Jesus. Today our body is the temple and habitation of God's Spirit.

## THE BELIEVER'S ANOINTING

1 John 2:20

1 John 2:27

When you make Jesus Christ your Lord and you become born again, God, the Holy Spirit, comes to live in you. God's presence comes to dwell in you and take up residence. THEREFORE, you are anointed.

There is an anointing that comes with the New Birth.

- When I am Born Again, I receive the Holy Spirit **WITHIN** me.
- When I am Baptized in the Holy Spirit, I receive the Holy Spirit **UPON** me.
- Every believer is ANOINTED to be a MINISTER of RECONCILIATION.

*"He who believes in Me, as the Scripture has said, out of his heart will flow rivers of living water."*

**John 7:38**

The "rivers of living water" is the anointing of God.

Your life should not be empty, dry, and void of the power of God. It will be if you sit and watch T.V. all day, or run around "busy" with the affairs of life or socializing, and never spend time with God in prayer and in the Word. Spend time waiting on God, fellowshipping with Him.

# Keys To The Anointing

**PERSONAL NOTES**

Acts 6:4 was the secret behind the success of the early church.

Acts 6:4 is the secret of the anointing today.

Acts 6:4 is the key to a ministry of miracles, signs, and wonders.

Are you willing to pay the price to walk daily in the anointing?

**Kathryn Kuhlman said,** "It will cost you everything."

God will use anybody if they will just spend time with Him and be available for Him to use them. Remember, God doesn't want your ability. All He wants is your AVAILABILITY.

If you are willing to pay the price and spend time with God in prayer, fellowship, and worship, then a greater manifestation of the anointing will flow in you and through you.

Stephen was in the ministry of helps, yet he flowed in God's supernatural power.

*"And Stephen, full of faith and power, did great wonders and signs among the people."*

Acts 6:8

Philip was a deacon, yet look at how greatly God used him.

Acts 8:5-8

There is a price to pay.

What is the price?

* You have to deny yourself.
* You have to wait on God.
* You have to die to your plans and obey God's plans.
* You have to lay aside your will and follow God's perfect will.
* You have to pray, fast, seek God, worship Jesus, and live a holy, consecrated life.
* You have to live in obedience to the voice of God in your life.

So, every believer is anointed by reason that the Holy Spirit dwells **within** and **upon** them.

## THE MINISTRY OF HELPS ANOINTING

**Romans 12:3-8**

There is an anointing that is on the ministry of helps – that refers to every believer who is not called to the Five-Fold Ministry of Apostle, Prophet, Evangelist, Pastor, and Teacher.

The ministry of helps refers to deacons, ushers, home cell leaders, musicians, psalmists, intercessors, counselors, church workers, and helpers in the church, etc.

Acts 6:2-7

Do you see the difference between the five-fold ministry and the ministry of helps? The

# Keys To The Anointing

ministry of helps is an essential ministry for the church today. It carries the supernatural anointing to be a servant.

There is an anointing to sing – not natural talent – but Holy Spirit ability.

Anointed music, and anointed praise and worship creates a platform and cultivates the atmosphere for miracles to take place.

## THE FIVE-FOLD MINISTRY ANOINTING

### Ephesians 4:11-16

Who God appoints, He anoints.

We must be God anointed, not man appointed.

The five-fold ministry gifts are:

(1) **APOSTLES**

(2) **PROPHETS**

(3) **EVANGELISTS**

(4) **PASTORS**

(5) **TEACHERS**

The purposes of the five-fold ministry are:

* **For the equipping of the saints for the work of ministry.**
* **For edifying and building up the body of Christ.**

We are SAINT "EQUIPPERS" and supernatural "BODY BUILDERS."

We need to expect the anointing to flow and place a demand on it each time we minister.

Give the anointing the opportunity to flow. MINISTER to people as God directs you. Don't just preach for two hours and sit down.

As God's five-fold ministers, we must have a reality of Acts 6:4 in our spirits and act on it because:

* **Your prayer life is essential.**
* **Your study of God's Word is vital.**

PRAYER and THE WORD are the DIVINE COMBINATION that will take your ministry forward in a NEW ANOINTING.

The key is for you to find out from God your place and your ministry in the body of Christ and then function there.

Find out what you are called to do and then **follow that calling. The anointing will follow you.** The anointing goes along with your calling.

If you are not anointed to do it, then there is no point in trying to pretend you are.

# Keys To The Anointing

There are levels and grades of anointing in the offices of ministry.

For example:

If you are called as a five-fold teacher, as you obey that calling and stick with it diligently, progressively the Lord will increase the anointing upon your ministry with a greater and heavier anointing in that office. However, that does not give you the license to step into or trespass into another office of ministry.

DO NOT COVET ANOTHER MAN'S CALLING OR MINISTRY.

Stay in the place and ministry where God has called you to function in the body of Christ.

## THE HAND OF GOD

The Bible speaks of THE HAND OF GOD or THE FINGER OF GOD, which is a reference to the anointing of God coming upon someone for a specific situation.

*"But if I cast out demons with the finger of God, surely the kingdom of God has come upon you."*

**Luke 11:20**

*"'But now bring me a musician." Then it happened, when the musician played, that the hand of the Lord came upon him."*

**2 Kings 3:15**

*"Then the hand of the Lord came upon Elijah; and he girded up his loins and ran ahead of Ahab to the entrance of Jezreel."*

**1 Kings 18:46**

The hand of the Lord – the anointing – can come upon you to do a specific thing, at a specific time, in a specific situation to achieve specific results.

(a) When God gifts you, calls you, and anoints you for MINISTRY, it is real and it remains with you. It stays. It abides even regardless of your personal walk with God.

*"For God's gifts and His call are irrevocable – He never withdraws them when once they are given, and He does not change His mind about those to whom He gives His grace or to Whom He sends His call."*

**Romans 11:29 (AMP)**

(b) The anointing is received sovereignly from God when He calls you into a specific ministry.
God anoints whoever He wants to anoint.
The anointing is the sovereign work of God, given and based upon the grace of God.
Man cannot achieve it, work it up, hype it up, and man cannot give it to you.

# Keys To The Anointing

**(c)** The anointing can be imparted and transferred from one man of God to another ONLY if the Holy Spirit leads and sovereignly directs, e.g.:

- Moses to Joshua
- Elijah to Elisha

**(d)** In the office God has called you into; you can covet, desire and go after a greater anointing in your ministry, a greater intensity and a deeper dimension of the anointing, to stand in your office.

*"And so it was, when they had crossed over, that Elijah said to Elisha, 'Ask! What may I do for you, before I am taken away from you?' And Elisha said, 'Please let a double portion of your spirit be upon me.'"*

2 Kings 2:9

Don't stop going after God until you have received the full anointing in your ministry.

Know what it is you are called to do, and obey that calling. Stay with it and move into all the anointing of that call and ministry.

Without the anointing, all the work, all the time spent in study, all the effort is fruitless and useless. We are just spinning our wheels!

**Without the anointing, everything is wasted effort.**

**Without the Holy Spirit, we have nothing to give people.**

**Without the anointing, our sermons are empty, dead words.**

**Without the anointing, we are helpless to do anything.**

We must rely 100% on the Holy Spirit, and have faith in the anointing to get the job done!

**Smith Wigglesworth said,** "God wants us to have THIN HEADS and FAT HEARTS."

It is far better to speak ten words, under the anointing and by the unction of the Holy Spirit, than ten thousand without Him.

## THE ANOINTING DESTROYS EVERY YOKE

*"It shall come to pass in that day, that his burden will be taken away from your shoulder, and his yoke from your neck, and the yoke will be destroyed because of the anointing oil."*

Isaiah 10:27

ALL YOKES:

Spiritual, physical, emotional, religious, financial, matrimonial, mental, demonic, sin, sickness, disease, oppression, fear, poverty, strife, lack, etc.

ARE DESTROYED.

**What is a yoke?**

# Keys To The Anointing

**PERSONAL NOTES**

It is any kind of power, influence, force, or addiction that puts you or holds you in bondage.

It can be sin, fear, bad habits, addictions, compulsive desires, sickness, poverty, etc.

**The anointing of God destroys:**                    **Isaiah 10:27**

- the yoke of religious tradition
- the yoke of deception
- the yoke of fear and depression
- the yoke of sin
- the yoke of sickness
- the yoke of unforgiveness and resentment
- the yoke of guilt and condemnation
- the yoke of demonic oppression
- the yoke of lust and pornography

*"Then Jesus, being filled with the Holy Spirit, returned from the Jordan, and was led by the Spirit into the wilderness."*

**Luke 4:1**

The Holy Spirit empowered and anointed Jesus for supernatural ministry.

Jesus had His faith tested by Satan during the wilderness experience. If He had given in to Satan, He would have come out of the wilderness defeated. But, because of the power of the Holy Spirit, He was victorious.

*"Then Jesus returned in the power of the Spirit to Galilee, and news of Him went out through all the surrounding region."*

**Luke 4:14**

His fame started in the wilderness, when He conquered Satan. After that, His fame kept spreading.

*"How God anointed Jesus of Nazareth with the Holy Spirit and with power, who went about doing good, and healing all that were oppressed of the devil, for God was with Him."*

**Acts 10:38**

Jesus acknowledged His power and results to the Holy Spirit.

## THE ANOINTING IS FOR ACTION

*"The Spirit of the Lord is upon Me, Because He has anointed Me To preach the gospel to the poor; He has sent Me to heal the brokenhearted, To proclaim deliverance to the captives And recovery of sight to the blind, To set at liberty those who are oppressed."*

**Luke 4:18**

# Keys To The Anointing

Through the anointing and power of the Holy Spirit, Jesus was able to:

**(1) Preach the Gospel to the poor** – message of prosperity

This includes:

a) The poor and feeble of the world.

b) Those who have nothing and are sick.

c) The rich of the world who, though they have everything materially, are in a state of lack and live in misery, because what they have does not satisfy them....they are spiritually poor.

**(2) Heal the brokenhearted** – message of healing

This speaks of people who have had their lives crushed by problems, have no answers, and as a result are in despair, in desperation, overcome with difficulties.

**(3) Preach deliverance to the captives** – message of deliverance

People who are captives and are held prisoner by forces stronger than they are. These forces which control them may be in the form of fear, habits, compulsive desires, addictions, or other bondages of sin. Often it can be the result of demonic influence.

**(4) Give sight to the blind** – message of restoration

Whether it be physical or spiritual blindness, both kinds can be healed by the power of the Holy Spirit.

**(5) Give liberty to the oppressed** – message of freedom

That is freedom from being crushed, hurt, and wounded ... spirit, soul, and body! Jesus did no healings, no miracles, no deliverances until He was anointed with the Holy Spirit at the age of 30 years. Before He was thirty, there were NO MIRACLES, NO HEALINGS, NO SIGNS AND WONDERS because He was not anointed.  It is the anointing that destroys the yoke.

*"And they were all amazed and said to one another, What kind of talk is this? For with authority and power He commands the foul spirits, and they come out!"*

Luke 4:36 (AMP)

*"Now at the setting of the sun [indicating the end of the Sabbath], all those who had [any that were] sick with various diseases brought them to Him, and He laid His hands upon every one of them and cured them. And demons even came out of many people, screaming and crying out, You are the Son of God! But He rebuked them, and would not permit them to speak, because they knew that He was the Christ, the Messiah."*

Luke 4:40, 41 (AMP)

# Keys To The Anointing

**PERSONAL NOTES**

If Jesus had to be anointed to preach the Gospel, to teach God's Word, to heal the sick, to cast out demons, and release miracles to set suffering mankind free, then you and I need the anointing of God today!

When Jesus left this earth, He legally transferred the anointing that was on Him and put it on us.

**Matthew 28:18-20**

**John 17:18, 20-22**

**John 20:21**

*"How God anointed Jesus of Nazareth with the Holy Spirit and with power, who went about doing good and healing all who were oppressed by the devil, for God was with Him."*

**Acts 10:38**

Child of God, remember, it is the **anointing that makes the difference.**

# LESSON: 4

# Releasing The Anointing

**PERSONAL NOTES**

**KEY VERSE:**   2 Corinthians 1:21  *"Now He who establishes us with you in Christ and has anointed us is God."*

**KEY TRUTH:**   As joint heirs with Christ, God has equipped us and anointed us with the same anointing Jesus walked in.

## HOW TO ACTIVATE THE ANOINTING

The anointing does not depend on your natural or professional abilities.  In fact, Scripture says:

**The anointing changes us into another man.**

*"Then the Spirit of the Lord will come upon you, and you will prophesy with them and be turned into another man."*

1 Samuel 10:6

You stop being a natural man and become supernatural.  Here are some keys to activating the anointing in your life.

**KEY NUMBER 1:**   Your Prayer Life.        Acts 2:4, 42

Acts 3:1

Acts 4:29-31, 33

The power of God is energized in us as we regularly pray – not religious praying – but Holy Ghost praying.

Jude 20

**KEY NUMBER 2:**   By Acting on the Word of God.

Luke 1:37

Mark 16:20

There is power in the Word of God when you believe it and act on it.

**KEY NUMBER 3:**   Exercising Your Faith in the Name of Jesus.

Acts 3:1-8, 16

Acts 4:7-10

**KEY NUMBER 4:**   The Anointing is Released Through Us When We Have Compassion and a Genuine Desire to Help People.

Matthew 14:14

Jesus was moved with compassion and love for the people and their needs. That is a key to moving in the anointing.

Moving with compassion causes you to move in the anointing.

# Releasing The Anointing

© 1994 The Believer's School of Training, Rev. Norman K. Robertson

**PERSONAL NOTES**

Compassion is a key to the anointing.

Paul said in **2 Corinthians 5:14**, *"The Love of God controls me."*

*"...This is the commandment, as you have heard from the beginning, that you continue to walk in love guided by it and following it."*

2 John 6 (AMP)

The divine flow of love releases the divine flow of the anointing.

**Read** the Gospels extensively and walk with Jesus through them.

**Study** His ministry of healings, miracles, and deliverances.

**See** what Jesus did. Follow His ministry and do what He did.

Be moved with compassion and love to meet the needs of people supernaturally through the power of God.

## KEY NUMBER 5: The Anointing is Released Through Laying Your Hands on the Sick.

Mark 16:17, 18

The anointing of God is imparted through laying on of hands.

Our hands are the hands of Jesus extended, transmitting the anointing of God to meet the needs of people.

Through the body of Christ, the Church, the hands of Jesus are extended to the sick, demonized, and oppressed.

## KEY NUMBER 6: Walking in Boldness Releases the Anointing.

Acts 4:13, 29-31

There is a DIVINE CONNECTION between the release and transference of the anointing and boldness. You have to be bold!

*"The wicked flee when no one pursues, But the righteous are bold as a lion."*

Proverbs 28:1

If you believe God has called you and anointed you to be a minister, then you should be bold about it. Bold in soulwinning! Bold against Satan and demons! Be bold to lay hands on people! Be bold against sickness, fear, and oppression!

Just be bold about it. Tell the people.

God has anointed you to heal the sick. God has anointed you to lay hands on them!

Boldness is not arrogance. Boldness means DARE TO DO.

Acts 3:1-6

# Releasing The Anointing

*"Then Peter said, 'Silver and gold I do not have, but what I do have I give you: In the name of Jesus Christ of Nazareth, rise up and walk.'"*

Acts 3:6

"WHAT I HAVE I GIVE YOU."

Peter had something to give.  It was the anointing. Peter gave the sick man something.

Acts 3:6-16

Acts 4:1-13

Notice **Verse 13:**

**Boldness** is something you can see.

**Boldness** has nothing to do with education.

**Boldness** is a key to releasing the anointing.

**Boldness** comes from spending time with Jesus.

Acts 3:6

Acts 3:16

Acts 4:13

We need to pray and ask the Holy Spirit to burn everything out of us that is not Jesus, so that Jesus can be clearly seen.  **Pray:** "God, let people see Jesus in me!"

## WALKING IN GOD'S ANOINTING

### A. THE WORD OF GOD

If we are to know God's anointing regularly and constantly, we must be a disciplined reader of the Word of God. We should set aside part of each day for this purpose, preferably first thing in the morning. We should ask the Lord to teach us, by the Holy Spirit, from His Word and to enlighten some part of the Word for us each day. Feeding on God's Word daily puts power in our inward man.

### B. PRAISE AND WORSHIP

Where there has been praise and worship from the heart to God it is very common for the anointing to be sensed. We should enter His courts with praise and as we do so and worship God, He makes His presence felt. It is not uncommon during praise or worship for the anointing to fall upon some person or persons in the gathering and for them to receive their healing.  Praise and worship create the platform for the flow of God's anointing.

### C. SALVATION

When I make an altar call, as people come forward to give their lives to Jesus Christ in public and confess His name, I often sense a powerful anointing upon the meeting.

# Releasing The Anointing

## D. WHEN THERE IS HEALING AND DELIVERANCE FROM DEMONS

When the signs following the ministry of God's Word are occurring, such as physical and emotional healing, demons being cast out, and other New Testament occurrences are taking place, then the power of God's anointing falls continually in such a situation.

## E. TESTIMONY

When somebody is testifying concerning God's dealings in their life or of their healing or deliverance, an anointing will frequently fall upon the meeting.

## F. PREACHING THE WORD

When the preacher or Bible teacher believes from his heart the Word of God and knows the power of the Holy Spirit in his life, particularly through the baptism with the Holy Spirit, then it is common for the anointing to fall in the meeting as he preaches. The preacher will himself know that anointing as he reads from the Scriptures and preaches the Word. It is as though he is receiving direction from God. Many times as I preach or teach, I feel the anointing fall as though the Lord is saying, "Yes, that is right, you are saying the truth, the right thing, to my people."

As we preach the uncompromised Word of God and teach in accordance with that Word, we should often feel that anointing fall upon us, confirming that we are teaching in accordance with God's will.

## G. MOVING IN THE GIFTS OF THE HOLY SPIRIT

When a believer or minister is operating in the Word of Knowledge, the Word of Wisdom, or Discerning of Spirits and the people sense the Holy Spirit's power present, then the anointing of God falls.

## H. PRAYER AND FASTING

Many times during prayer and fasting the anointing of God can be felt.

## I. WALKING IN THE WILL OF GOD

When all our thoughts and actions are centered on God through Jesus Christ and we are seeking to follow His will, whether it be in the work place or elsewhere, we can frequently sense the anointing of God upon us.

## J. WHEN TWO OR MORE ARE GATHERED IN THE NAME OF JESUS CHRIST

When there is a gathering of believers committed to the Lordship of Jesus Christ or who are seeking such commitment and begin to put aside all doubt, fear, and unbelief, then the anointing of God falls on the gathering. As fellowship grows and the people listen to the preaching and teaching given by an anointed teacher, then the power of God can literally be felt in the place.

# Releasing The Anointing

## K. REPENTANCE

It is an attitude of repentance towards God that enables Him to anoint us afresh with the power of His Holy Spirit.

Acts 3:19

# WE NEED THE ANOINTING

If there was ever a time when we needed the anointing of God, it is now.

In the same way as Jesus Christ did not commence His ministry until the Holy Spirit came upon Him and anointed Him for service, so we need the full power of the Holy Spirit in our lives, and this same anointing. All believers should know their inheritance in God and the anointing which He has already given them.

Child of God, it is when we earnestly seek the face of God in whatever circumstances and cast aside all doubt, fear, and unbelief, that His presence can be known physically to us as the anointing.

It is true that we walk by faith and not by sight or by our feelings, but I am confident that if we do truly walk by faith, then we shall know the feeling of the anointing of God.

We must become sensitive to the anointing in our life.

1 John 2:20, 27

**The anointing is the presence of God in manifestation.**

At times you can feel the anointing of the Holy Spirit coming upon you like a physical power or presence of God — it can come as a warm sensation, a heat, a glow, or else at times you can feel the wind of the Spirit.

It is important to PRACTICE the presence of God and become consciously aware of the anointing of God.

## DIFFERENT OCCASIONS WHEN THE ANOINTING IS SENSED:

(1) During praise and worship

(2) Reading the Word of God

(3) Preaching and teaching the Word of God

(4) When ministering healing to the sick

(5) When the vocal gifts operate
   e.g. Prophecy is going forth in a church service

(6) During times of prayer and intercession, waiting on God

(7) When God uses you in the gifts of the Spirit

(8) When praying for one another you can feel or sense the presence of God

# Releasing The Anointing

**PERSONAL NOTES**

## THE ANOINTING IS TANGIBLE AND TRANSFERABLE

*"But Jesus said, "Somebody touched me, for I perceived power going out from me.""*

Luke 8:46

**NOTICE:** Jesus knew someone had touched Him with faith, because He "perceived" healing power – the anointing – go out from Him.
When power was released from Jesus, He knew it.
When the healing anointing went out from Jesus, He knew it. He was conscious of it. It is TANGIBLE.

How do you "perceive" God's anointing?

There will be times when your body will react to it. You will feel WARMTH, HEAT, TINGLING ELECTRICITY. People fall under the power.

Sometimes when you preach or teach, you feel as if you are "wearing a cloak" as you minister God's Word.

When people fall under the power, it is a DISPLAY OF GOD'S ANOINTING manifested.

- Abraham fell under the power of God when the blood covenant was cut with El Shaddai.

- Daniel became weak at the knees and fell under God's power when the angel of the Lord visited him.

- When Jesus ministered to people, sometimes they fell under the power of God, e.g., the lunatic boy.

- When Jesus was betrayed by Judas Iscariot and they came to arrest Him, He spoke and they were knocked down and fell back under God's power.

- When Saul of Tarsus was converted to Christ on the Damascus road, he fell under the power of God.

Jesus did not base His ministry on whether people fell down or not. However, many times I have laid hands on people and have felt the flow of God's anointing go through my hands, yet they have resisted it!

Don't rebel, resist, or fight against God's anointing. Yield to the anointing.

God's anointing is TANGIBLE and it can be TRANSMITTED.

**Laying on of hands is a Spiritual Law.**

Jesus, in His ministry, laid His hands on sick people:

The Leper (Matthew 8)

The Woman with the Spirit of Infirmity for 18 years (Luke 13)

The Two Blind Men (Matthew 20)

In these healing miracles and others, Jesus "touched" or laid His hands upon the sick people in obedience to spiritual laws.

# Releasing The Anointing

The power of God, the healing anointing, the "DUNAMIS" virtue of the Holy Spirit flowed through the hands of Jesus into the bodies of sick people to destroy the works of the devil and cure them.

## THE LAW OF CONTACT AND TRANSMISSION

Jesus was anointed with God's healing power.
Luke 4:18

Acts 10:38

The contact of the hands of Jesus upon the sick caused a transfer or transmission of God's healing anointing to go into the body of the sick person to undo the works of the devil, destroy the disease, and to effect a healing and a cure in their body.

There are spiritual laws that govern your receiving of healing in your body.

Matthew 14:35, 36

In other cases of healing, the sick "touched" Jesus and the "DUNAMIS HEALING VIRTUE" within Jesus went out from Him. It was transmitted into the bodies of the sick people as they touched Him in faith.

The faith of the sick people touching Jesus was the connection that "TAPPED" the healing anointing in Jesus and caused the flow of virtue into their bodies.

This is the law of contact and transmission in operation.

Acts 19:11, 12

The LAYING ON OF HANDS was the "conductor" that released and transmitted the anointing of God from Paul into aprons and handkerchiefs. These become "storage batteries" for God's anointing and healing virtue, to be taken to the sick and demon oppressed.

- Jesus' hands, words, and clothes were carriers and conductors of God's anointing.

- Elijah's mantle was a carrier and conductor of God's miracle power.

- Elisha's bones, even though he was dead, were a storage battery for the anointing of God.

- Moses' rod was a conductor of God's power.

- Peter's shadow was a carrier and a conductor of God's power.

- Pauls' aprons and handkerchiefs were carriers and conductors of the anointing.

## TRANSMITTING THE ANOINTING

The anointing of God, radiating and emanating from Paul into his clothes and handkerchiefs, became "storage batteries" for God's anointing.

Acts 19:11,12, tells us:

(1) The anointing of God is tangible and real.

(2) The anointing of God is capable of being stored and transferred.

(3) The anointing of God causes sicknesses, diseases, and demons to depart.

# Releasing The Anointing

**PERSONAL NOTES**

If you don't believe in the anointing and the law of contact and transmission, then it won't work for you. Jesus, in His hometown, was resisted with unbelief and doubt and could do no miracles there.

**Mark 6:1-6**

Faith in the anointing of God – belief in the power of laying on of hands – can release God's miracle power into your body.

The anointing is like power inside a storage battery. It can be stored and it can be discharged! The anointing can be renewed in your prayer closet, as you spend time in the Father's presence.

The anointing is tangible and has many conductors.

The anointing can be "transmitted and transferred" through various conductors.
CONDUCTOR = POINT OF CONTACT:

- Through LAYING ON OF HANDS
- Through SPEAKING WORDS
- Through CLOTHES and HANDKERCHIEFS

The anointing was present in the life and ministry of Jesus, but it only benefited those who believed He was anointed.

*"Now it happened on a certain day, as He was teaching, that there were Pharisees and teachers of the law sitting by, who had come out of every town of Galilee, Judea, and Jerusalem. And the power of the Lord was present to heal them."*

**Luke 5:17**

Do you know that the Bible only records ONE MAN – the paralyzed man – that day in that crowd, who received healing and was ministered to by the anointing?

The anointing had NO EFFECT on the majority of the people, even though God's power to heal was there! The Pharisees and religious people present didn't believe that Jesus was anointed.

Read and study Mark 6:1-6

Unbelief and doubt stop the power of God operating and stop the anointing from being released. (Mark 6:5)

A bad attitude will quench the anointing of the Spirit of God.

There are different methods the Holy Spirit uses as "CONDUCTORS" for God's anointing:

- Moses' Rod
- Elijah's Mantel

# Releasing The Anointing

- Elisha's Staff

- Jesus' Hands, Words, and Clothes

- Peter's Shadow

- Paul's Handkerchiefs and Aprons

All of them were conductors of the anointing. Your openness, attitude, and reception to the anointing is vital for it to work.

## WOMAN WITH THE ISSUE OF BLOOD

**Mark 5:25-34**

- This sick woman had a strong confession of faith in Jesus, the Healer.

- This sick woman not only had a confession, but she had corresponding actions backing up what she said with her mouth.

- Touching the garment of Jesus was the point of contact she established to release her faith. She was convinced that she would receive healing for her condition the moment she touched Jesus' clothing.

- Her faith in Jesus placed a demand on the healing power of God in Jesus, and that healing anointing flowed from Jesus into her to cure her condition!

- The anointing of God is a tangible substance. It can be felt and it can be transmitted.

**From Mark 5 we learn the following:**
**NUMBER 1:**
Jesus perceived, he knew the healing anointing had left Him and gone into someone.

**Mark 5:30**

**NUMBER 2:**
The woman's faith "tapped" or placed a demand on the anointing of Jesus.

**Mark 5:27, 28, 34**

**NUMBER 3:**
The woman "felt" the tangibility of the anointing go into her sick body.

**Mark 5:29**

**NUMBER 4:**
The anointing destroyed the yoke of sickness in her body. She was cured of a disease of twelve years.

**Mark 5:29, 34**

**NUMBER 5:**
The conductor that carried Jesus' anointing was His clothes.

**Mark 5:28**

# Releasing The Anointing

## FOUR PRINCIPLES ABOUT THE ANOINTING FROM MARK 5

(1) The anointing is TANGIBLE.

(2) The anointing is TRANSFERABLE. It can be transmitted.

(3) Faith puts a demand on the anointing of God.

(4) The anointing destroys the yoke of Satan and sickness.

## THE TANGIBLE ANOINTING

The anointing can be released, it can be transmitted. It can leave you and enter the sick or oppressed to free them.

As a minister, I spend a lot of time praying in the Spirit. You release the anointing by praying much in tongues. Jude 20 tells us that we build up our spirits with God's anointing, strength, and power by praying in the Holy Ghost.

Lay hands on the sick and tell the people God has anointed you.

The minister's hands today are like the hem of Jesus' garment.

**Tell the people you are ministering to:**

- "The LAYING ON OF HANDS IS YOUR POINT OF CONTACT TO RECEIVE."

- "When I lay my hands on you, I am giving you something you need. TAKE IT. RECEIVE IT. I am giving you the healing anointing. God's power will drive out your pains and cure your sicknesses. Don't fight it. Receive it."

- "I am not the healer. Jesus is."

- "I am not the baptizer in the Holy Spirit. Jesus is."

- "All I am is the channel, the vessel, the instrument in God's hands."

- "It is God's power and God's anointing. All I do is deliver it. I allow it to flow through me into you!"

"As I lay my hands upon you, I expect God's anointing to flow and cause miracles, signs, wonders, healings, deliverances to take place!"

The anointing can diminish. It can be used up. It can be drained as you give it out to people who put a demand on it. That is why you must replenish or renew the supply of the anointing regularly.

Jesus had to do this. He did it through His consistent prayer life, early in the morning or through all night communion and fellowship with the Father.

Luke 5:16, 17

Mark 1:35-37

Luke 6:12, 17-19

# Releasing The Anointing

The anointing is like TALENTS:

The more you use it to bless others and the more you use it to establish the Kingdom of God, then the more anointing God will give you.

You cannot break bondages over people's lives without the anointing.

*"It shall come to pass in that day that his burden will be taken away from your shoulder, And his yoke from your neck, And the yoke will be destroyed because of the anointing oil."*

Isaiah 10:27

Paul, the Apostle, realized the importance of the anointing.

*"And my speech and my preaching were not with persuasive words of human wisdom, but in demonstration of the Spirit and of power."*

1 Corinthians 2:4

## PROFESSIONAL UNANOINTED OR ANOINTED UNPROFESSIONAL?

Intellectual sermons don't get the job done.

Entertainment from the pulpit doesn't set people free.

There are **professional unanointed people** in the church who preach, sing, and try to minister but there is no anointing.

AND

There are **unprofessional anointed people**

who do not have oratory skills,

who do not have talented musical abilities,

who do not have great communication abilities,

But they do have the anointing!

Having the anointing is really what counts.

Without the anointing, no demonic yokes will be destroyed.

Without the anointing, there is no equipment to get the job done.

It is time to become sensitive to the presence and power of God manifest.

It is time to be sensitive to the anointing.

**Quoting from Brother John Willison, in** *Balm of Gilead* **Magazine:**

"A heavy anointing of God in manifestation in our lives and ministries will cause:

- Saving knowledge to increase
- Secure sinners to be awakened
- Dead souls to live

# Releasing The Anointing

© 1994 The Believer's School of Training, Rev. Norman K. Robertson

**PERSONAL NOTES**

- Hard hearts to be melted
- Satan's strongholds to be pulled down
- Strong lusts to be broken
- Ministries to be lively
- Unity in the church
- Our prayer life to be powerful
- Healings and real miracles to take place
- The Gospel light to shine clear
- Conviction of the vileness of sin
- Great additions to the "Kingdom of God"

If we really had the anointing we are supposed to have, then we would really see in manifestation the New Testament results we are supposed to have!

## BLOCKAGES TO THE FLOW OF THE ANOINTING

**(1) People having no respect and no reverence for God and for the moving of His Spirit.**

**Hebrews 12:28, 29**

So often, we come to church full of T.V., full of strife with our family, and full of bad attitudes.

We sit in church with our mind on our lunch, our business, the golf course, our watch. "Let's see what the preacher is going to do today."

The Big Question is:

**Are you serving God for what you can get or are you serving God because you love Him?**

Some Christians, the only time they pray is SHOPPING LIST PRAYERS. "GIMME, GIMME, Lord, my name is Jimmy."

**(2) Unholy living, or living in strife with people.        2 Timothy 2:19-23**

The time has come for the body of Christ to walk in purity and unity. We must live right. Sin always weakens the anointing.

**(3) Not spending time in God's Word and in prayer.        Matthew 4:4**

**2 Timothy 2:15**

**2 Timothy 3:16,17**

- You need the Word of God in your life – DAILY BREAD.
- You need to fellowship with God in prayer every day.

**(4) Neglecting the gifts of God in your life will hinder you.**

**1 Timothy 4:14-16**

# Releasing The Anointing

Remember the parable of the talents. You must use, exercise, and put to work what God has invested in your life.

2 Timothy 1:6

Use your gifts! "Use it or lose it" is a Biblical principle.

**There are 21 New Testament Gifts for the New Testament Church.** Find your place and gift and function for the glory of God. The anointing follows your calling. When you find your calling then you will find your anointing.

**(5) Allowing yourself to become "entangled" in the affairs of this life will hinder the anointing.**

2 Timothy 2:3, 4

Watch out for and guard yourself against the cares of this life:

WORK CARES                    MONEY CARES                    MINISTRY CARES

Read and study Mark 4:14-20

The devil and your flesh can get you to a place where you are "fragmenting" yourself and your time in all kinds of directions – works of wood, hay, and stubble.

Don't make money a priority.

JESUS SAID, "MY YOKE IS EASY AND MY BURDEN IS LIGHT."

**(6) Another blockage to the anointing is not respecting the ministry gifts that God has set in the Church.**

Ephesians 4:11, 12
1 Corinthians 12:27, 28

In Jesus' hometown, He could not move in miracle power or the healing anointing because of the bad attitudes of people.

Mark 6:1-6
1 Timothy 5:17

**(7) Another hindrance to the flow of the anointing is compromising the message of God's Word and the moving of the Holy Spirit because you want to be an accepted, popular preacher.**

2 Timothy 4:1-4

**(8) A lack of faithfulness is a hindrance to the anointing. Be faithful to your call and ministry.**

- HOW HUNGRY ARE YOU FOR GOD?

- HOW THIRSTY ARE YOU FOR THE ANOINTING?

- HOW DESPERATE ARE YOU FOR THE MOVING OF THE HOLY SPIRIT?

# Releasing The Anointing

**PERSONAL NOTES**

## HOW EVERY CHRISTIAN CAN HAVE A SUPERNATURAL MINISTRY

Isaiah 8:18          Mark 16:17, 18          John 14:12          Acts 1:8

Every covenant child of God is to move in signs and wonders and flow in the supernatural anointing of God. This was true in the Old Testament and in the New Testament.

We are to supernaturally:

- Speak in tongues

- Minister to the sick

- Cast out demons

- Operate in the gifts of the Spirit

- Preach the Gospel with power

- Do the works of Jesus

**1 Corinthians 12: 1, 7-11, 31**

To move in the supernatural and see God moving through us and operating through us, we must be willing to get out of the boat and walk on the water. Supernatural ministry involves risk taking.

When it comes to moving in the supernatural power of God, flowing in the gifts of the Spirit, we must not play it safe. We must step out in faith and risk making mistakes. Peter walked on the water to Jesus. The other eleven disciples played it safe.

## KEYS TO MOVING IN THE POWER OF GOD

### KEY NUMBER 1

**You must believe that you are the person God says you are.**

**1 Peter 2:9, 10**

- not what the devil says you are.

- not what you think you are from a natural standpoint.

- not what other people say you are.

- not what you feel you are.

### SAY:

"I am strong in the Lord and not weak.

God's anointing is upon my life to set people free.

I am full of the Holy Ghost and Fire."

# Releasing The Anointing

## YOU ARE A NEW TESTAMENT BELIEVER

- Righteous in Christ
- A new creation – Partaker of God's divine nature
- Full of the Holy Spirit
- Anointed of God
- The greater One lives in you
- A king and a priest
- Forgiven, cleansed, saved, and redeemed by the blood of Jesus
- You can do all things through Christ
- Indwelt by the Holy Spirit, able to move in the divine gifts of the Holy Spirit
- Bold as a lion, without condemnation
- Living in divine health
- Free from fear, weakness, inferiority
- Strong in the Lord and operating in supernatural energy
- Led by the Holy Spirit and walking in the wisdom of God
- Possessing the mind of Christ

The New Testament believer is a powerful force for God!

You must have a revelation of your potential in Christ.

**Believe you are the person God says you are.**

**Believe who you are in Christ.**

**Know what you have in Christ.**

**Act on what you can do through Christ.**

Find your place in the body of Christ. Know what your ministry is. Start to function supernaturally where God wants you.

## KEY NUMBER 2

**Believe you are where God says you are.**                    Colossians 1:13, 14

- You are no longer in Satan's kingdom.
- You are now living in the Kingdom of God, washed in the Blood of Jesus.
- You are delivered from the power of darkness, Satan.
- You are living in the Kingdom of light.

Know your place in the body of Christ. Find out where you fit in and be a blessing where God has planted you.

# Releasing The Anointing

© 1994 The Believer's School of Training, Rev. Norman K. Robertson

**PERSONAL NOTES**

## KEY NUMBER 3
**Believe you can do what God says you CAN DO and start DOING IT.**

Luke 4:18
Mark 16:17, 18
1 Corinthians 12:7-11

- Decide to act on what the New Testament says.
- Declare what you can do in Christ, then start doing it.
- Put into action what you know the Bible teaches.
- I can do all things through the abilities of Christ in me.
- I can cast out demons IN JESUS' NAME.
- I can heal the sick IN JESUS' NAME.
- I can prophesy the word of the Lord and edify the church.
- I can do the same works that Jesus did.
- I can minister with the power of the Holy Spirit.
- I can flow in the gifts of the Spirit.
- I can hear the voice of God with accuracy.
- I can move in the supernatural Word of knowledge.
- I can teach the Bible with power and authority.
- I can move in a signs and wonders ministry to set the captives free.
- I can witness for Christ with boldness.
- I can reach out and win the lost.
- I can be a blessing to someone in need.
- I can set the oppressed free in JESUS' NAME.
- I can serve the Lord effectively.
- I can walk in the Spirit.
- I can pray and read my Bible daily.
- God's anointing in me meets the needs of people around me.

*"...the people who know their God shall be strong, and carry out great exploits."*

**Daniel 11:32**

# Releasing The Anointing

## A PROPHECY: THE ANOINTING IS FOR EVERYONE

On September 26, 1993, the following prophecy was delivered by Pastor Rodney Lloyd while I was holding a week of Holy Ghost revival meetings in his church.

*"Many do not understand, sayeth the Lord, that I've anointed my whole church. I've not anointed this group or this group or this group. But it's My purpose, sayeth the living God, that the anointing be upon all of My true people. I put My anointing upon My Son, His name was Jesus. He was the body of Christ when He walked the face of the earth. Now you are the body of Christ, sayeth the Lord. And the anointing that I put upon Him is the same anointing, the same Holy Spirit is upon My church. But many would say, I don't sense the anointing, I don't feel the anointing, I don't know the anointing, I don't flow in the anointing. I would declare unto you, sayeth the living God, that My Son pressed in to Me, My Son sought Me, My Son was about My business. What business are you about, sayeth the living God? I would declare unto you that those that have gone before, the fathers of the church, the Apostles, those subsequent to them, they were about My business. They sought Me. What are you seeking? What are you about? It is those that are hungry for me that get my touch. It is those that are thirsty for Me that experience Me in great measure. My anointing goes upon the whole body. If they're open to it, there's enough ministry to go around. No one has a corner on the market of ministry. The anointing is for everyone. My spirit was poured out for the whole church. Seek Me. Be hungry for Me. Be thirsty for Me. Be about My business, sayeth the Lord, and you will experience My touch, you'll experience My anointing. Hunger for the things of the world, thirst for the things of the world, be busy with those and you will not experience My anointing, but there will be an increasing anointing of deception upon you from the enemy Satan and he'll deceive you more and more and rather than pressing in to Me, you'll be pulled out further from My presence and you'll walk away from Me and you'll be left in destruction. This is an hour, sayeth the Lord, that My people must be about My business. This is an hour, sayeth the Lord, that My people must choose. They must reorder their lives, they must allow Me to have My way for their good for My glory. Then you'll know what the anointing is all about, sayeth the living God."*

# Response To Truth
*Lessons 3 and 4*

**IMPORTANT:** *Take time this week to review the powerful lessons on the anointing. As you meditate on these truths, ask the Holy Spirit to increase your awareness and sensitivity to the flow of the anointing in your life.*

© 1994 The Believer's School of Training, Rev. Norman K. Robertson

**PERSONAL NOTES**

## KEY QUESTIONS

(1) List five blockages to the anointing flowing through a believer's life.

(2) The anointing is both tangible and transferable. Explain this.

(3) How do we go about activating the anointing today?

(4) What is the difference between the ministry of helps anointing and the five-fold ministry?

(5) Explain being an ANOINTED UNPROFESSIONAL versus being an UNANOINTED PROFESSIONAL.

(6) What are three vital keys to moving in the power of the Spirit?

## MEMORY WORK

Psalm 92:10

1 Corinthians 2:4, 5

1 John 2:20

## PERSONAL APPLICATION

(1) How often do you sense the quickening of God's anointing in your life as you read the Word? Pray? Attend church services? Pray for people's needs?

(2) Will you pay the price to receive a greater anointing upon your life and ministry?

## RECOMMENDED READING

Kenneth E. Hagin, *Understanding the Anointing*

Kenneth E. Hagin, *A Fresh Anointing*

Benny Hinn, *The Anointing*

Rodney M. Howard-Browne, *The Touch of God*

# LESSON: 5                     Divine Healing Truths For Today

© 1994 The Believer's School of Training, Rev. Norman K. Robertson

**KEY VERSE:**   Matthew 8:16,17   *"When evening had come, they brought to Him many who were demon-possessed. And He cast out the spirits with a word, and healed all who were sick, that it might be fulfilled which was spoken by Isaiah the prophet, saying: 'He Himself took our infirmities and bore our sicknesses.' "*

**KEY TRUTH:**   God's will is and always will be HEALING AND HEALTH for His people. It's as much His will to heal the sick as it is to save the lost. Healing of men's bodies is as much a part of God's redemptive nature as saving men's souls.

## COMMON QUESTIONS ABOUT SICKNESS AND HEALING

(1)  Where does sickness come from?

(2)  Is it God's will to heal today?

(3)  Did Jesus pay for our healing at the cross?

(4)  How does God heal today?

(5)  Why do some people fail to receive healing?

(6)  How can I receive healing from God?

Jesus said in John 8:31, 32, "You will know the truth and knowing the truth will make you free."

Jesus said in John 17:17, "Father, sanctify your people through your truth – your Word is truth."

As we look at the subject of Divine healing and health we want the Bible to be our only textbook.

- Not philosophy.

- Not human experience.

- Not religious doctrines.

- Not the traditions of men.

- Not your ideas or my opinions.

Because if you don't know the Truth then you won't be free.

*"Beloved, I pray that you may prosper in all things and be in health, just as your soul prospers."*

3 John 2

# Divine Healing Truths For Today

**PERSONAL NOTES**

The Holy Spirit says that God's highest desire and will for your life is health.

## WHAT DOES THE BIBLE SAY ABOUT SICKNESS?

- Sickness is called CAPTIVITY. People who are sick are prisoners of the devil. **Job 42:10**
- Jesus calls sickness a SPIRIT OF INFIRMITY. **Luke 13:11**
- God's Word calls sickness SATANIC BONDAGE. **Luke 13:16**
- The Bible calls sickness OPPRESSION of the devil. **Acts 10:38**
- The Bible calls all sickness and disease EVIL. **Deuteronomy 7:15 (AMP)**
- The Bible says that all sickness is A CURSE. **Deuteronomy 28:15-68**

This is how God's Word describes sickness:

(1) CAPTIVITY

(2) SPIRIT OF INFIRMITY

(3) SATANIC BONDAGE

(4) OPPRESSION OF THE DEVIL

(5) EVIL

(6) A CURSE

These are six Biblical definitions of sickness.

## WHERE DOES SICKNESS COME FROM?

Sickness is not from God because sickness and disease were not part of God's original plan for man.

*"Then God saw everything that He had made, and indeed it was very good. So the evening and the morning were the sixth day."*

**Genesis 1:31**

When God made Adam and Eve, they were made perfect in the image of God (is God sick?) and they lived in divine health because there was no sickness in the Garden of Eden before the fall.

*"Then God said, 'Let us make man in Our image, according to Our likeness; let them have dominion over the fish of the sea, over the birds of the air, and over the cattle, over all the earth and over every creeping thing that creeps on the earth.'"*

**Genesis 1:26**

# Divine Healing Truths For Today

Sickness and disease came upon the human race only after man sinned.

*"Therefore, just as through one man sin entered the world, and death through sin, and thus death spread to all men, because all sinned..."*

Romans 5:12

Sickness came into this earth on the heels of spiritual death.

Sickness is the forerunner of death. Disease is the death process begun.

**John Alexander Dowie said**, "Sickness and Disease is the foul offspring of its Mother, Sin and its Father, Satan."

## THE ORIGIN OF SICKNESS

**The late E. W. Kenyon, a powerful Bible teacher, explained it this way:**

"It is hard for us to understand that the laws that are governing the earth very largely came into being with the fall of man, and with the curse upon the earth.

It is because of this that many accuse God of the accidents that take place, of the sickness and death of loved ones, of storms and catastrophes, of earthquakes and floods that continually occur.

They came with the Fall. Their author is Satan, and when Satan is finally eliminated from the earth, these laws will stop functioning. "

Jesus' description of the Father and His declaration that 'He that has seen me has seen the Father', makes it impossible for us for a moment to accept the teaching that disease and sickness are of God.

The Father's very nature refutes the argument that He would use sickness to discipline us or to deepen our spiritual life. God, our Heavenly Father, is not a child abuser.

Jesus plainly taught us in Luke 13 in speaking of the woman with the infirmity, that disease is of the devil.

If you will read carefully the four Gospels, you will notice that Jesus was continually casting demons out of sick people, breaking Satan's dominion over the lives of men and women.

In Acts 10:38, Peter tells us, *Jesus of Nazareth, how God anointed Him with the Holy Spirit and with power: who went about doing good, and healing all that were oppressed of the devil; for God was with Him.*

In the Great Commission Jesus said, *"These signs shall accompany them that believe: in my name shall they cast out demons; they shall speak with new tongues; they shall take up serpents, and if they drink any deadly thing, it shall in no wise hurt them; they shall lay hands on the sick, and they shall recover."*

There is no such thing as the separation of disease and sickness from Satan.

Disease came with the fall of man.

Sickness and sin have the same origin.

Two books of E. W. Kenyon which I strongly recommend are: *Jesus the Healer* and *New Creation Realities.*

# Divine Healing Truths For Today

© 1994 The Believer's School of Training, Rev. Norman K. Robertson

**PERSONAL NOTES**

## BIBLE PROOF THAT SICKNESS IS SATAN'S WORK

(1) Satan smote Job with sore boils.                    **Job 2:7**

(2) God turned the captivity of Job.                    **Job 42:10**

(3) Man possessed with a blind devil.                   **Matthew 12:22**

(4) Satan bound the daughter of the Covenant.           **Luke 13:16**

(5) *"The thief does not come except to steal, and to kill, and to destroy. I have come that they may have life, and that they might have it more abundantly."*

**John 10:10**

(6) *"How God anointed Jesus of Nazareth with the Holy Spirit and with power, who went about doing good and healing all that were oppressed of the devil, for God was with Him."*

**Acts 10:38**

(7) *"Deliver such a one to Satan for the destruction of the flesh..."*

**1 Corinthians 5:5**

(8) *"And they cast out many demons, and anointed with oil many who were sick, and healed them."*

**Mark 6:13**

(9) *"...through death He might destroy him who had the power of death, that is, the devil."*

**Hebrews 2:14**

(10) *"...the Son of God was manifested, that He might destroy the works of the devil."*

**1 John 3:8**

The works of the devil come about by demon spirits causing disease.

God's Word clearly teaches us that:

- Sickness is never sent by God or used by God to chastise or discipline His children or to make them better Christians.

- Sickness was never part of God's original plan. It came as a result of the fall.

- Sickness is a curse of the broken law, the penalty for living in disobedience to God's Word.

- Sickness and the work of demon spirits are connected. They go hand in hand.

# Divine Healing Truths For Today

It is not God's will for any of His children to suffer with sickness and disease. The Father stated His will clearly when He sent Jesus to the cross to take our sins and sicknesses.

Never in the Bible is sickness viewed as something good. Some have tried to see disease as a blessing, a tool in God's hand which He uses to purge us and mold us. But this kind of concept is alien to the Scriptures.

Sickness in the Bible is called:

* Satanic captivity

* Satanic bondage

* Satanic oppression

* A curse

Sickness is a curse from the devil – an enemy of man and God.

This is just how Jesus looked at sickness. He viewed it as a form of oppression. His desire was to set men free from this and every other kind of bondage.

Sickness is the work of Satan which came about as a result of man's fall. It is not the will of God.

For centuries the enemy has told the lie that God wants His children to be bound up with illness and disease. Unfortunately, the church as a whole has believed it.

Sickness and disease don't come under the heading of suffering for Jesus' sake. (If that were true, then only Christians would be sick.) If a believer is physically ill, he is not suffering for Jesus. He is being oppressed by the enemy, and Jesus has paid the price to set him free.

## THE HEALING COVENANT

God is a Healing God and He established a Healing Covenant in the Old Testament.

*"...If you diligently heed the voice of the Lord your God and do what is right in His sight, give ear to His commandments and keep all His statutes, I will put none of the diseases on you which I have brought on the Egyptians. For I am the Lord who heals you."*

                                                                    Exodus 15:26

*"So you shall serve the Lord your God, and He will bless your bread and your water. And I will take sickness away from the midst of you. No one shall suffer miscarriage or be barren in your land; I will fulfill the number of your days."*
                                                                    Exodus 23:25,26

*"And the Lord will take away from you all sickness, and will afflict you with none of the terrible diseases of Egypt which you have known, but will lay them on all those who hate you."*

                                                                    Deuteronomy 7:15

# Divine Healing Truths For Today

**PERSONAL NOTES**

God's Healing Covenant states:

(1) Exodus 15:26     **I will not permit sickness to touch your body.**

(2) Exodus 23:25     **I will take away all your sickness.**

(3) Deuteronomy 7:15  **I will take away from you all the diseases of "EGYPT".**

This includes every disease in the world today.

*"But now He has obtained a more excellent ministry, inasmuch as He is also Mediator of a better covenant, which was established on better promises."*
                                                        **Hebrews 8:6**

*"He also brought them out with silver and gold, And there was none feeble among His tribes.*
                                                        **Psalm 105:37**

In the great Exodus deliverance from Egypt, when God brought out His people, there was not one FEEBLE, SICK, WEAK, TIRED or DISEASED person among over three million people.

This should be the same experience with the body of Christ today because in the New Covenant we have a better covenant with better promises.

**READ: Deuteronomy 7:9-15**

Notice carefully the Blessings and the Divine Promises God gives to His Covenant Children:

(1) God is the faithful covenant-keeping God who guarantees to bless His children.

(2) God loves you and it is His will to bless you and multiply you (confer prosperity upon you.)

(3) Your children will be blessed.

(4) Your business (career, job, company) will be blessed and prosperous.

(5) You will be blessed ABOVE all people (highly favored, prosperous, victorious, and successful).

(6) You will not be barren (husband/wife), but you will be fruitful in bringing forth children.

(7) The Lord will TAKE AWAY FROM YOU all sickness and all disease – divine healing. This speaks about PHYSICAL DELIVERANCE!

(8) The Lord will deliver and protect you from all the diseases of Egypt – divine health.

(9) Anybody who rises up against you with HATRED will suffer sickness. They will get sick.

# Divine Healing Truths For Today

Here, the Bible shows us that Christians can call judgement upon those who HATE the church or oppose the work of God.

God has promised us not only divine healing, but divine health.

*"So you shall serve the Lord your God, and He will bless your bread and your water. And I will take sickness away from the midst of you. No one shall suffer miscarriage or be barren in your land; I will fulfill the number of your days."*
Exodus 23:25, 26

This is a covenant guarantee and the condition is IF YOU SERVE THE LORD (not play around with sin, not rebel, not murmur against God).

**God says:**      **I will bless your bread and your water.**

**I will take all sickness away from you.**

**I will fulfill the number of your days.**

This is a covenant promise of divine health and long life and it is for every child of God today.

*"Moses was one hundred and twenty years old when he died. His eyes were not dim nor his natural vigor diminished."*
Deuteronomy 34:7

Moses lived a long life. He died strong and healthy.

*"And now, behold, the Lord has kept me alive, as He said, these forty-five years, ever since the Lord spoke this word to Moses while Israel wandered in the wilderness; and now here I am this day, eighty-five years old. As yet I am as strong this day as on the day that Moses sent me; just as my strength was then, so now is my strength for war, both for going out and for coming in."*
Joshua 14:10, 11

Both Caleb and Joshua lived a long, healthy, strong life.

Abraham, Moses, and Joshua died healthy. They lived and died in PERFECT HEALTH.

God wants all of His children to live in health and die in good health.

*"You shall come to the grave at a full age, As a sheaf of grain ripens in its season."*
Job 5:26

Start claiming this Scripture. "Full age" means a healthy, full age.

*"They shall still bear fruit in old age; They shall be fresh and flourishing."*
Psalm 92:14

God has promised you and me health – divine health –and a long life all of our days.

# Divine Healing Truths For Today

**PERSONAL NOTES**

*"My covenant I will not break, Nor alter the word that has gone out of My lips."*
Psalm 89:34

This is talking about God's healing covenant.

*"No evil shall befall you, Nor shall any plague come near your dwelling; For He shall give His angels charge over you, To keep you in all your ways."*
Psalms 91:10, 11

**God has promised us protection from sickness. He says, "NO SICKNESS WILL COME NEAR YOU!"**

*"Beloved, I pray that you may prosper in all things and be in health, just as your soul prospers.*
3 John 2

God promised us health, long life, and even IMMUNITY from all sickness and disease, and God is not a liar.

*"Who satisfies your mouth with good things, So that your youth is renewed like the eagle's."*
Psalm 103:5

Healing is part of the character of God and He never changes.
Healing is in God's nature and He never changes.
The Lord God was the Healer in the Old Testament.

*"...For I am the Lord who heals you."*     Exodus 15:26

*"Who forgives all your iniquities, Who heals all your diseases."*
Psalm 103:3

Notice:          He forgives "all" our iniquities.
                 He heals "all" our diseases.
"All" means everything. All is all and that is all there is to it!

**Psalm 103:4 (in the Septuagint Translation of the Scripture) says:**
*"God is constantly, consistently, and continually keeping health in your body and redeeming your body from destructive diseases."*

**Exodus 15:26 gives us four basic instructions for health.**

(1) Diligently hearken or "give heed" to the Word of God. This means to hear the Word and speak it. Declare it.

(2) "Do" what is right. Actively respond by doing what the Word of God says to do.

(3) "Give ear" to God's Commandments, God's Words, means to make a commitment to what you hear.

# Divine Healing Truths For Today

(4) "Keep" all His statutes – live in obedience to the Word of God – means to guard, protect, and preserve.

**By living by these four instructions,** God's healing covenant promises:

"I am the Lord your Healer and I will not permit any sickness to touch your body."

**(1) Hear the Word of God and confess it (Quote Scripture).**

**(2) Apply the Word of God in your life by acting on it.**

**(3) Make a commitment to what you hear.**

**(4) Protect the Word in your heart.**

## THE REDEMPTIVE NAMES OF GOD

"Jehovah" is distinctly the redemption name of deity.

Seven times in the Old Testament, the name "Jehovah" is joined with another Hebrew word to form a compound name. These seven compound names each reveal a distinct aspect of God's redemptive nature. They are:

| | |
|---|---|
| **Jehovah-Rapha,** meaning the Lord that heals. | **Exodus 15:26** |
| **Jehovah-Jireh,** meaning the Lord will provide. | **Genesis 22:13, 14** |
| **Jehovah-Nissi,** meaning the Lord our banner or victory. | **Exodus 17:15** |
| **Jehovah-Shalom,** meaning the Lord our peace. | **Judges 6:24** |
| **Jehovah-Raah,** meaning the Lord our shepherd. | **Psalm 23:1** |
| **Jehovah-Tsidkenu,** meaning the Lord our righteousness. | **Jeremiah 23:6** |
| **Jehovah-Shammah,** meaning the Lord is ever present with us. | **Ezekiel 48:35** |

**Dr. C. I. Scofield has said:**

"In His redemptive relation to man, Jehovah has seven compound names which reveal Him as meeting every need of man from his lost state to the end."

When the Lord joined His own name to the word "Rapha", which means healer or healing, He was not just saying that He would or could heal.

He was saying "My name IS Healer!" It meant that healing is actually part of God's redemptive nature.

Jesus was Jehovah-Rapha in flesh and blood form.

Through Him, God displayed to the world His healing nature. Jesus revealed that the Father wants people to be free from the oppression of sickness and disease.

The Lord has always made provision for healing and health for His covenant people. This is true under both the Old and New Covenants.

Under the Old Covenant, God promised to remove all sickness from the children of Israel if they remained faithful to Him.

Under the New Covenant, Jesus Himself bore our sicknesses and pains as part of His redemptive work on the cross.

# Divine Healing Truths For Today

**PERSONAL NOTES**

## WHAT IS DIVINE HEALING?

Divine healing is God acting supernaturally, by the power of the Holy Spirit, causing the human body to be healed, cured, and delivered from sickness and its power so the body is made whole and restored to health and soundness.

## FOUR PILLARS OF TRUTH ABOUT DIVINE HEALING

**NUMBER 1**   God revealed Himself in the Old Testament as our healer and Great Physician.

> Exodus 15:26
> Exodus 23:25, 26
> Deuteronomy 7:14, 15

By nature, God is a healing God who is against sickness and disease.

> Psalm 103:2-4
> Psalm 105:37
> Psalm 107:20

God is the healer of the physical body. This is a cardinal fact of the Old Covenant.

**NUMBER 2**   God, revealed in the person of Jesus, came as the healer of sick, suffering humanity.

> Matthew 4:23, 24
> Matthew 9:35
> Matthew 11:4, 5

Over seventy percent of the earthly ministry of Jesus was spent in healing the sick, casting out demons, performing miracles, and laying hands on people.

> Matthew 8:1-3, 5-9, 13-17, 28-33

Jesus came to reveal God the Father, His will, and His nature to mankind.

> Hebrews 1:1-3

Jesus came as 'EMMANUEL' – God with us – and healed all who were sick and oppressed by the devil.

> Acts 10:38

Jesus was God in a human body and clearly showed that God was the healer of the human race.

Jesus is not the oppressor. He is the healer. God reveals Himself through Jesus, as the healer of mankind.

Read the four Gospels. Read the life and ministry of Jesus in Matthew, Mark, Luke, and John, and you will see it is clearly God's will to heal people.

**NUMBER 3**   God revealed himself as healer through the New Testament church. The New Testament church was a healing church.

> Acts 4:29-31

# Divine Healing Truths For Today

God's plan, purpose, and blueprint for the church is revealed in the twenty-eight chapters of the Book of Acts.

Divine healing and physical miracles manifested through the New Testament church.

Acts 3:1-8, 16 ..........................................Healing of the crippled beggar.

Acts 5:14-16 ...........................................Healing of multitudes in the streets of Jerusalem.

Acts 8:5-7 ...............................................Healing and miracles in Samaria.

Acts 9:32-34 ...........................................Aeneas miraculously healed after being paralyzed for eight years.

Acts 14:8-10 ...........................................Crippled man healed by the power of God.

Acts 19:11, 12 ........................................Healing through anointed prayer cloths.

Acts 28:1-9 .............................................Various healings take place on the island of Malta.

**<u>NUMBER 4</u>**   **God has placed GIFTS of Healings in the church and given the church today the ministry of healing.**

> **1 Corinthians 12:7-9, 28**
>
> **James 5:14-16**

James 5:14 states that God will heal ANYONE who is sick with ANY KIND of sickness. Jesus commanded His twelve disciples to heal the sick.

> **Matthew 10:1, 7, 8**
>
> **Luke 9:1, 2, 6**

Jesus commissioned the seventy disciples to heal the sick.   **Luke 10:1, 9, 17-20**

God has appointed men and women in the church whom He has endued with special power over diseases. The gift of healings refers not to an individual receiving healing from God, but rather to God's empowering men to heal, and then placing them in the body of Christ.

Sovereignly the Lord anoints believers to heal specific areas of the body (eyes, ears, backs, etc.). That's why this spiritual gift is plural – "gifts of healings." This is not a generalized power to heal.

This is a specific anointing, for a specific need, at a specific time.

This gift is manifested as the Spirit wills, and not as men will. It is entirely up to God how or when this gift is going to operate. Very often, the person who receives by this means has operated little or no faith. God has sovereignly moved on his behalf.

# Divine Healing Truths For Today

© *1994 The Believer's School of Training, Rev. Norman K. Robertson*

**PERSONAL NOTES**

Jesus has commissioned every believer, the entire church today, with the ministry of healing.

John 14:12

Matthew 28:18-20

Mark 16:17, 18

## DIVINE HEALING IN THE BIBLE

(1) God, in the Old Testament, showed Himself as the healer of the physical body.

(2) God, manifested in the flesh through Jesus, healed the sick.

(3) The New Testament church was a healing church.

(4) God has set healing gifts in the body of Christ.

These cardinal facts are the Biblical basis for the healing ministry.

Charles T. Studd, a great pioneer missionary during the early part of this century, told how he and a companion rediscovered the power of divine healing.

While engaged in missionary work in the jungles of Central Africa, Studd contracted a deadly form of jungle fever. He steadily grew worse as the days passed. None of the available medicine had any effect.

Then, when all hope seemed lost, the Spirit brought to his mind James' words to the sick, "Let them pray over him, anointing him with oil."

Although he had never heard of anyone being healed in this way, he and his partner decided to take God at His Word.

Because they were in the middle of the jungle, their supplies were limited. The only oil they had was the kerosene in their lamps.

But it made no difference. Studd was anointed with kerosene and God healed him!

The very next day, he was able to get up and continue his work among the African tribes.

## TEN WAYS GOD CAN HEAL YOUR BODY

God wants us to be healed so much that He has made at least ten ways available for us to get healed.

(1) God has put gifts of healings in the New Testament church.                                    1 Corinthians 12:9

(2) Anointing the sick with oil.                         James 5:14, 15

(3) Healing through prayer cloths (special anointing).                                         Acts 19:11, 12

(4) Praying the prayer of agreement.            Matthew 18:18, 19

(5) By speaking words of faith (saying it).     Mark 11:23

# Divine Healing Truths For Today

(6) Laying on of hands — transmitting the
anointing of God.                Mark 16:18

(7) Praying the prayer of faith.          Mark 11:24

(8) Using the name of Jesus to resist sickness
and Satan.                       John 14:12, 13
                                       James 4:7

(9) Taking God's Word as medicine through
meditating healing Scriptures.         Psalm 107:20
                                       Proverbs 4:20-22

(10) By receiving the Lord's Supper in faith.     1 Corinthians 11:23-30

## WHY SOME PEOPLE FAIL TO RECEIVE PHYSICAL HEALING

### REASON NUMBER 1

Lack of knowledge of God's Word about healing.

*"My people are destroyed for lack of knowledge..."*     Hosea 4:6

*"And you shall know the truth, and the truth shall make you free."*
                                       John 8:32

### REASON NUMBER 2

Unforgiveness, resentment, strife, and bitterness in their life.

*"And whenever you stand praying, if you have anything against anyone, forgive him, that your Father in heaven may also forgive you your trespasses. But if you do not forgive, neither will your Father who is in heaven forgive your trespasses."*

                                       Mark 11:25, 26

### REASON NUMBER 3

Fear, worry, and a negative confession about their condition after being prayed for.

*"Casting all your care upon Him, for He cares for you."*
                                       1 Peter 5:7

*"Let us hold fast the confession of our hope without wavering, for He who promised is faithful."*

                                       Hebrews 10:23

# Divine Healing Truths For Today

**PERSONAL NOTES**

## REASON NUMBER 4

Believing the traditions of men and the lies of the devil.

*"Making the Word of God of no effect through your tradition which you have handed down. And many such things you do."*

**Mark 7:13**

NOTICE: Jesus taught that men's traditions are more powerful than God's Word!

**The tradition of men teaches:**

(1) Pray, if it be thy will, concerning healing.

(2) Paul's thorn in the flesh was sickness and sometimes God will use sickness as a thorn in our flesh.

(3) God uses sickness to discipline and chastise His children.

(4) The suffering of Job is for the church. What he went through, so do we.

(5) Sometimes God is glorified by your sickness – being sick is saintly.

(6) Healing is not always the will of God, for God moves in mysterious ways.

(7) Healing and miracles have passed away.

(8) God heals only those people that it is His will to heal. He does not heal everybody.

## DIVINE HEALING MEDICINE

The Word of God is "Healing Medicine" for your physical body.

**Proverbs 4:20-22**

God's divine healing medicine is listed here. This is God's remedy – Gods' prescription for a healthy body.

Reading, studying, confessing, and meditating in God's Word will bring health to all your flesh.

We've all probably experienced a visit to the doctor's office at some time in our life. When he found out what was wrong, the doctor usually prescribed some kind of medicine to assist our body's own healing processes.

The medicine bottle we got from the pharmacist came with explicit instructions, telling us when to take it and how much to take.

God has His own prescription for healing, a medicine that works on every kind of disease, no matter how incurable that disease may be.

God's medicine is His WORD.

The Word is LIFE to those who find it, and HEALTH to all their flesh. The Hebrew word for health can also be translated MEDICINE. God's Word is medicine to our flesh – that is, our physical bodies.

# Divine Healing Truths For Today

© 1994 The Believer's School of Training, Rev. Norman K. Robertson

God's medicine comes complete with instructions on how and when to take it. But it is up to us to follow the directions. The Word is only life and health to those who find it. We have to be diligent to do what God says if we are to reap the benefits of what He has provided.

No matter how effective a prescribed medicine may be, it won't do any good until it is taken as directed.

Imagine if a patient were to call his doctor, complaining that his medicine was not working.

The doctor asks, "Are you taking it as you are supposed to?"

The patient replies, "No, but I've got it right here beside my bed."

This seems foolish. Medicine does not do any good on your nightstand. You've got to take it before it will help you.

Many Christians do exactly the same thing with God's medicine.

Instead of taking it as directed, they leave it on the shelf. When asked "Are you reading and meditating on the Word (God's medicine)..."

They answer, "No, but I carry it with me everywhere. I even sleep with it under my pillow."

The only way God's medicine will do us any good is if we take it as God Himself has directed.

These are the directions for taking God's medicine, His Word:

## Proverbs 4:20-22

### (1) Give attention to God's Word.

We must give the Word first place in our lives. Before we listen to anything else, we should see what the Bible has to say.

With regard to healing, this means paying more attention to God's promise in the Scripture than to the physical symptoms or the doctor's report.

### (2) Incline your ear to God's Word.

Incline means "leaning toward" or "stretching," as if to hear better what is being said. The image being portrayed here is one of leaning or stretching forward to be able to hear the words being spoken. We all do this from time to time. When we are intensely interested in what someone is saying, we lean toward the speaker so that we don't miss anything.

This is to be our attitude towards God's Word. We must hang on every word God speaks, inclining our ear so that we don't miss anything.

### (3) Don't let God's Word depart from your sight.

We can never get too much of God's medicine! There is no such thing as an overdose with the Lord's prescription.

# Divine Healing Truths For Today

**PERSONAL NOTES**

We should constantly feed our heart and mind with the Scripture. Not letting it out of our sight doesn't mean reading all the time. It simply means keeping our attention on the Word.

One of the best ways to do this is by speaking the Scriptures throughout the day, keeping it always in our "sight" (that is, our attention.)

**(4) Keep God's Word in the midst of your heart.**

This is the aim of the previous three instructions. We keep the Word in our heart by:

* giving attention.
* inclining our ear.
* not letting the Word out of our thoughts.

The directions for taking God's medicine are not complicated. In fact, they are very simple. But they must be followed DILIGENTLY!

**Proverbs 4:20-22**

The Word of God is health to all your flesh.

(1) **Pay attention to God's Word — your MIND.**

(2) **Listen to the Word — your EARS.**

(3) **Keep looking at what the Word says — your EYES.**

(4) **Keep the Scriptures at the center of your life — love the Word with your HEART.**

**Romans 10:17**

Faith comes by hearing and hearing by the Word.

Don't stop HEARING THE WORD. You have got to keep on hearing God's Word. It is a continuous action.

When the Word of God fills your life and saturates you, it will become health to all your flesh.

Total saturation of God's Words:

* Get God's Words in your EARS.
* Get God's Words before your EYES.
* Get God's Words into your HEART.

Notice: The Words of God are LIFE and HEALTH to all your flesh (skin, blood, muscles, bones, organs, eyes, ears, teeth, every tissue).

**E. W. Kenyon said,** "I believe it is the plan of the Father that no believer should ever be sick, that he should live his full length of time and actually wear out and fall asleep."

**Psalm 90:10**
**Job 5:26**

# LESSON: 6                                              God's Healing Power

**KEY VERSE:**      Psalm 107:20      *"He sent His word and healed them, And delivered them from their destructions."*

**KEY TRUTH:**      The Bible shows us that Jesus Christ purchased physical healing at Calvary, and that He did so for ALL, not just some. We can be certain that God never wants His children to suffer with disease, pain, or sickness.

## SIXTEEN BIBLE FACTS ABOUT SICKNESS AND HEALING

(1) Health was natural and eternal before the fall.          **Genesis 1:26-31**

(2) Both death and sickness originated with sin and are now being propagated by Satan.

**Romans 5:12-21**

(3) God made a healing covenant with His people to heal them of all diseases.

**Exodus 15:26, 23:25**
**Deuteronomy 7:15**

(4) Health as well as healing is promised when men meet God's conditions.

**Exodus 15:26**
**Deuteronomy 28**
**Psalm 91**
**3 John 2**

(5) Christ came to redeem us from both sin and sickness.

**Isaiah 53**
**Matthew 8:17**
**Galatians 3:13**
**Romans 8:2**
**Acts 10:38**
**1 Peter 2:24**
**1 John 3:8**

(6) Every disciple called and sent by Christ was given power to heal.

**Matthew 10:1-8**
**Mark 6:7-13**
**Luke 10:1-19**
**Acts 1:8**

# God's Healing Power

**PERSONAL NOTES**

(7)  All disciples throughout this present age are commanded to observe the same commands Christ gave the first disciples which include healing the sick.

> **Matthew 28:20**
> **Acts 1:4-8**
> **Mark 16:15-20**

(8)  The Holy Spirit was sent into the world to continue the healing ministry of Christ.

> **1 Corinthians 12**
> **Hebrews 2:3, 4**

(9)  Jesus promised every believer power to do the works that He did.

> **Mark 9:23**
> **John 14:12-14**

(10)  Gifts of healings and other supernatural gifts are promised as the spiritual equipment of the church.

> **1 Corinthians 12:1-11**
> **Hebrews 2:3,4**

(11)  Healing is provided as part of Christ's atonement.          **Isaiah 53:4,5**
> **Matthew 8:16, 17**

Healing is the children's bread and their promised right because of the Blood Covenant.

> **1 John 3:8**
> **Luke 13:16**
> **3 John 2**
> **Matthew 15:26**

(12)  Healing is one of the five supernatural signs of the Gospel to follow believers.
> **Mark 16:15-20**

(13)  Healing was not only for the Old Testament days...

> **Exodus 15:26**
> **Psalm 91**
> **Psalm 103:3**

...and for the millennium,

> **Isaiah 30:26, 33:24**

# God's Healing Power

it is also for this age, or the Gospel is faulty and the New Covenant worse than the old one.

> **Matthew 8:17**
> **Matthew 21:22**
> **Mark 9:23**
> **Hebrews 8:6**

**(14)** Healing is part of salvation, for the Hebrew and Greek words for salvation all mean forgiveness, healing, health, and full deliverance from the curse.

> **Romans 1:16**
> **Galatians 3:13**
> **1 Peter 2:24**

**(15)** Healing is received on the same basis as forgiveness of sins – prayer and faith.

> **James 1:4-8**
> **James 5:14-16**
> **Hebrews 11:6**

**(16)** Healing and forgiveness are inseparable realities of the Gospel.

> **Matthew 9:5**
> **Matthew 13:15**
> **Acts 3:16**
> **Acts 4:12**
> **Acts 28:27**

**KEY TRUTH:**      Faith begins where the will of God is known.
                      God's Word is His will and His will is His Word

Back in Bible days, Jesus never once refused to heal anyone who came to Him. All who came to Jesus in Bible days were healed, cured, and made well. All who touched Him were healed. All whom He laid His hands upon were made whole.

## WHY DOES SICKNESS COME UPON OUR BODIES?

There are three main reasons:

<u>NUMBER 1</u>      Because of SIN.

> **Deuteronomy 28:15,27,45**

Living in disobedience to God's Word brings the penalty of the curse.

<u>NUMBER 2</u>      Because of IGNORANCE. Lack of knowledge of God's Word.

> **Hosea 4:6**

Ignorance of God's Word will keep you sick. Ignorance is NOT bliss.

# God's Healing Power

© 1994 The Believer's School of Training, Rev. Norman K. Robertson

**NUMBER 3**      Because of UNBELIEF. Lack of faith in God's Covenant will give Satan the opportunity to put sickness on you.

## JESUS, OUR SICKNESS BEARER

Divine healing was and is covered in the Blood Atonement, the sacrificial death of Jesus on the cross.

**READ: ISAIAH 53:3-6;10-12** (See Dr. Young's translation and Dr. Isaac Lesser's translation)

- Was Divine healing covered in the shed blood on the cross?
- Was Divine healing covered in the sacrificial death of Christ?
- Is healing for the body available through the cross of Christ?

The Word of God is very clear and precise. At the cross, Jesus bore your sins so you could be forgiven, made righteous, and be born again.

The same blood that took your sins away also took your PAINS AND SICKNESSES away.

**Isaiah 53:4**

Divine healing is included and just as much a part of Christ's Blood Atonement as the forgiveness of our sins.

## A WORD STUDY OF ISAIAH 53

Verses 4, 12 – "BORNE"          **Hebrew "NASA"** means to suffer punishment for, to suffer the penalty for, to lift up, to carry away and remove to a far distance.

Verses 3, 4 – "GRIEFS"          **Hebrew "CHOLI"** means sicknesses and diseases and is translated that way all through the Old Testament.

Verse 4 – "CARRIED"          **Hebrew "SABAL"** means to bear something as a penalty.

Verses 3, 4 – "SORROWS"          **Hebrew "MAKOB"** means pains and afflictions.

By His shed blood, Jesus took upon Himself and He carried away all your sickness and pains at Calvary once and for all.

Believe your healing is in the blood.

**Isaiah 53:4, 5**

No pain belongs in your body.

No sickness and no disease belongs in your body.

The same blood that washed all your sins away also carried away all your PAINS, SICKNESSES, and DISEASES.

# God's Healing Power

Jesus, on the cross, shed His blood to bring us forgiveness of all of our sins and to bring us physical healing in our bodies.

There is forgiveness and healing in the blood of Jesus.

In Isaiah 53:4-6, Isaiah prophesied our healing on the cross in 700 B.C.

In 1 Peter 2:24, Peter looks back on the FINISHED work of Calvary.

All our pain, all our sickness, all our disease, all our physical affliction was laid upon Jesus at Calvary. What He bore, we don't have to bear in our bodies.

Deliverance from all sickness and healing for our body is ours today because of the cross of Jesus.

Isaiah foresaw the Lord's suffering on the cross, and saw that Jesus would carry sickness as well as sin. Jesus bore our sicknesses and carried our pains. By the stripes and scourgings which He suffered, we are healed.

## HEALING IN THE ATONEMENT

In Peter's mind, healing was an accomplished provision (1 Peter 2:24). Jesus did the work when He bore our diseases on the cross. And so Peter puts healing in the past tense. By His wounds you WERE healed. The work is completed; the price has been paid.

All we need to do is trust and receive what God has so freely provided for us. We don't need to beg God. We don't need to seek His will. He's already made COMPLETE PROVISION for our healing through His Son.

**Romans 8:2, 32**

If you have confidence in the effectiveness of the cross, you can have confidence that God has given healing to us.

### Isaiah Chapter 53

### Verse 3 (NKJ)

*"He is despised and rejected by men, A Man of sorrows and acquainted with grief. And we hid, as it were, our faces from Him; He was despised, and we did not esteem Him.*

### Verse 3 (Literal Hebrew)

*"Jesus Christ is despised and rejected by men. A man of pains (makob) and familiar with sickness (choli) and disease. We turned our backs on Him and looked the other way. He was despised and we didn't care."*

### Verse 4 (NKJ)

*"Surely He has borne our griefs and carried our sorrows; Yet we esteemed Him stricken, Smitten by God, and afflicted."*

# God's Healing Power

**PERSONAL NOTES**

### Verse 4 (Literal Hebrew)

*"Certainly He took all our pains, carried the burden of our sicknesses and our diseases were placed on Him. Yet we did esteem Him stricken, smitten by God and afflicted."*

### Verse 5 (NKJ)

***"But He was wounded for our transgressions, He was bruised for our iniquities; The chastisement for our peace was upon Him, and by His stripes we are healed."***

### Verse 5 (Literal Hebrew)

*"But He was wounded and bruised for our sins, the punishment needful to obtain peace, prosperity, and well being for us He suffered. By His bruises and stripes healing belongs to us."*

### Verse 6 (NKJ)

***"All we like sheep have gone astray; We have turned, every one, to his own way; and the Lord has laid on Him the iniquity of us all."***

### Verse 6 (Literal Hebrew)

*"Everyone of us like sheep have strayed away to follow our own ways, Yet God has placed on Him the guilt and sins of us all. "*

### Verse 10 (NKJ)

***"Yet it pleased the Lord to bruise Him; He has put Him to grief, When you make his soul an offering for sin."***

### Verse 10 (Literal Hebrew)

*"But it was God's will to crush Him through disease, He has placed on Him sickness and will make His soul an offering for sin."*

## Key Words in Isaiah 53:4, 5

### "Borne" Defined:

The idea is that of one person taking the burden of another and placing it on Himself. If Christ bore our sicknesses, then they were taken away in the same sense sins were taken away, or borne, in verses 4 and 11.

### "Carried" Defined:

The idea is that the full load is taken by the one carrying it so that all others might be free of it. The meaning is that Christ bore all our sicknesses and pains, so that we do not need to have them; and if we do have them it is because we have not unloaded them on Him, by faith.

# God's Healing Power

**References in making atonement:**

a) **Wound - Hebrew "chalal",** to wound; to pierce. This refers to piercing the hands, feet, side.

b) **Bruise - Hebrew "daka",** to beat to pieces; break; bruise; crush. This refers to the stripes by scourging, cuts by thorns, and other bodily sufferings; and proves this was part of the work of atonement by which blood was shed. It was by this particular phase of punishment that bodily healing was provided for all.

*"I gave My back to those who struck Me, And My cheeks to those who plucked out the beard; I did not hide My face from shame and spitting."*

Isaiah 50:6 (NKJ)

*"Just as many were astonished at you, so His visage was marred more than any man, and His form more than the sons of men."*

Isaiah 52:14 (NKJ)

*"Yet many shall be amazed when they see Him - yes, even far-off foreign nations and their kings; they shall stand dumbfounded, speechless in His presence. For they shall see and understand what they had not been told before. They shall see my Servant beaten and bloodied, so disfigured one would scarcely know it was a person standing there."*

Isaiah 52:14 (Living)

*"The plowers plowed on my back; they made their furrows long."*

Psalm 129:3 (NKJ)

*"Though my back is cut to ribbons with their whips."*

Psalm 129:3 (Living)

*"...By whose stripes you were healed."*          1 Peter 2:24

## WHAT WE CAN LEARN FROM ISAIAH CHAPTER 53

(1) Jesus Christ our Lord was despised and rejected by men.

(2) At the cross, Jesus as our substitute became our sin-bearer and sickness-bearer.

(3) Jesus was made sin and sickness for all mankind.

(4) Jesus took all our pain and carried away the full load of our sicknesses.

(5) At the cross, all our diseases were placed on Jesus.

(6) Jesus was wounded and bruised for our sins.

(7) Jesus was punished to obtain peace and well-being for us.

(8) By the stripes of Jesus, sound health is ours.

(9) At the cross, God placed on Jesus all of our sins to make us RIGHTEOUS in Him.

# God's Healing Power

**PERSONAL NOTES**

(10) At the cross, God placed on Jesus all of our sickness and all our diseases to cure us, heal our bodies, make us physically whole, and restore us to SOUND HEALTH.

*"For the husband is head of the wife, as also Christ is head of the church; and He is the Savior of the body."*

Ephesians 5:23

**The Bible specifically states that Jesus Christ is the SAVIOR of the body:**

* Jesus delivers and saves us from SIN and SICKNESS.
* Freedom from all sickness, disease, and infirmity belongs to us IN CHRIST.
* 1 Corinthians 6:13 tells us that the physical body is for the Lord and the Lord is for the body.
* The physical body is not for Satan, not for sickness, not for pain or affliction.
* The Lord is for my body, meaning He undertakes to protect my body and keep my body safe from the attacks of sickness.

1 Peter 2:24

On the cross Jesus became SIN with my sin.

Jesus became SICK with my sickness.

When Jesus hung on the cross all my sin and all my sickness hung on the cross with Him.

SALVATION - **"SOZO"**, a Greek word that means deliverance from sin and sickness.

Sin and sickness have the same root, and the same source, and the same remedy.

The price for our healing has already been paid. We don't have to pay again the debt that Jesus paid. We don't have to be sick with the sickness that He already bore.

**God doesn't want us to suffer with anything that Jesus suffered with on the cross.** What Jesus experienced at Calvary, He experienced so that we wouldn't have to.

The curse of sickness belongs to the old man:

* The fallen Adamic nature.
* The curse that came with the fall.

IT DOES NOT belong to the new man IN CHRIST.

Sickness and disease have no place in the body of a Christian, no part in the new creation inheritance.

There should be no sickness in the new creation family.

Legally, on the cross, the blood of Jesus delivered and transferred our spirit, soul and body from Satan's authority and the kingdom of darkness. That means NO MORE SICKNESS.

# God's Healing Power

*"He has delivered us from the power of darkness and translated us into the kingdom of the Son of His love, in whom we have redemption through His blood, the forgiveness of sins.*

Colossians 1:13, 14

We have redemption from all sickness through the power of Jesus' blood.

*"He also brought them out with silver and gold, And there was none feeble among His tribes."*

Psalm 105:37

Deuteronomy 7:13-15

You have the right, in Jesus' name, to break the power of barrenness in your marriage – the power to make you fruitful in bearing and bringing forth children.

*"And the Lord will take away from thee all sickness, and will put none of the evil diseases of Egypt, which thou knowest, upon thee; but will lay them upon all them that hate thee."*

Deuteronomy 7:15 (KJV)

**NOTICE:**

   (1) The Lord will take away from you all sickness.

   (2) Disease is EVIL.

The Bible calls disease evil.

All sickness and all disease is evil—that means from the devil and demons.

God only gives us GOOD THINGS, not evil things.

God states that if we will walk in obedience to His covenant, we will never get sick.

*"He sent His word and healed them, And delivered them from their destructions."*

Psalm 107:20

*"But if the Spirit of Him who raised Jesus from the dead dwells in you, He who raised Christ from the dead will also give life to your mortal bodies through His Spirit who dwells in you."*

Romans 8:11

*"That thy way may be known upon earth, thy saving health among all nations."*

Psalm 67:2 (KJV)

**"SAVING HEALTH"** is God's will for suffering mankind.

*"But He answered and said, It is not good to take the children's bread and throw it to the little dogs."*

Matthew 15:26

# God's Healing Power

**PERSONAL NOTES**

Healing is the **children's "BREAD".**

This means covenant benefits such as salvation from sin, sickness, poverty, fear, and Satanic bondage!

Matthew 1:21– "SAVE"

The **Greek** word, **"SOZO"** means full deliverance from sin and the effects of sin which include sickness and everything else that happened because of the fall.

God promises to take away from us all sickness and make us immune from all diseases.

Divine protection from all sickness and all disease belongs to us.

**Psalm 91:1-16**

## REDEEMED FROM THE CURSE OF SICKNESS

*"Christ has redeemed us from the curse of the law, having become a curse for us (for it is written, 'Cursed is every one who hangs on a tree').".*
**Galatians 3:13**

### A Study In Deuteronomy Chapter 28

**Verse 15 (NKJ)**

*"But it shall come to pass, if you do not obey the voice of the Lord your God, to observe carefully all His commandments and His statutes which I command you today, that all these curses will come upon you and overtake you."*

**Verse 15 (Literal Hebrew)**

*"If you refuse to obey God's Word and choose to live contrary to His principles then because of disobedience all these curses will come upon you and overtake you."*

**Verse 21 (NKJ)**

*"The Lord will make the plague cling to you until He has consumed you from the land which you are going to possess."*

**Verse 21 (Literal Hebrew)**

*"The Lord will permit a deadly disease to attach itself to your body until you are destroyed from the face of the land you are going to possess."*

   (1) The Plague or Pestilence refers to any type of epidemic such as flu, typhoid, cholera. It also refers to a deadly disease that produces a slow death, e.g., AIDS.

**Verse 22 (NKJ)**

*"The Lord will strike you with consumption, with fever, with inflammation, with severe burning fever, with the sword, with scorching, and with mildew; they shall pursue you until you perish."*

# God's Healing Power

### Verse 22 (Literal Hebrew)
*"The Lord will allow you to suffer tuberculosis, bronchitis, all kinds of fever, infectious diseases, cancer, malaria, jaundice, war, draught, and crop failure until you are destroyed."*

   (2)  Consumption refers to tuberculosis, bronchitis, asthma, emphysema, any wasting disease.

   (3)  Fever refers to all types of fever such as scarlet, typhus, smallpox, yellow and all eruptive fevers.

   (4)  Inflammation refers to ulcers, a rapidly consuming cancer or infectious disease.

   (5)  Severe burning fever refers to malaria.

   (6)  Mildew refers to jaundice.

### Verse 27 (NKJ)
*"The Lord will strike you with the boils of Egypt, with tumors, with the scab, and with the itch, from which you cannot be healed.*

### Verse 27 (Literal Hebrew)
*"The Lord will allow you to suffer in your body with syphilis, tumors, ulcers, hemorrhoids, and all types of skin complaints for which there is no remedy."*

   (7)  Boils or the Botch of Egypt refers to syphilis, venereal disease, all sexually transmitted diseases.

   (8)  Emerods or Tumors refers to all types of tumors, ulcers, or hemorrhoids.

   (9)  Scab and the itch refers to all types of skin diseases and skin problems – e.g., acne, eczema, skin cancer, warts, etc.

### Verse 28 (NKJ)
*"The Lord will strike you with madness and blindness and confusion of heart."*

### Verse 28 (Literal Hebrew)
*"The Lord will allow you to suffer mental oppression, insanity, all kinds of eye problems, blindness, fear, and nervous breakdown."*

   (10)  Madness refers to insanity, and oppression of the mind and thought life, mental disorders, inability to think clearly.

   (11)  Blindness refers to all types of eye complaints, cataracts, glaucoma, etc.

   (12)  Confusion of heart can mean attacks on your nervous system and nervous breakdown.

# God's Healing Power

**PERSONAL NOTES**

**Verse 35 (NKJ)**
*"The Lord will strike you in the knees and on the legs and with severe boils which cannot be healed, and from the sole of your foot to the top of your head."*

**Verse 35 (Literal Hebrew)**
*"The Lord will allow you to be covered with boils from head to foot and you will suffer arthritis."*

(13) Sickness in the knees and in the legs can refer to arthritis, rheumatism, bone problems, stiff joints.

(14) Severe boils or sore botch refers to sores and boils all over the body which cannot be healed. Can also be leprosy.

**Verse 59 (NKJ)**
*"Then the Lord will bring upon you and your descendants extraordinary plagues – great and prolonged plagues – and serious and prolonged sicknesses."*

**Verse 59 (Literal Hebrew)**
*"The Lord will permit deadly epidemics to come on you and your children – also you will suffer with chronic sickness and lingering ailments in your body that will go on for years."*

(15) Extraordinary plagues refers to deadly epidemics and incurable diseases.

(16) Serious and prolonged sicknesses refers to chronic sicknesses and ailments of long duration.

**Verse 60 (NKJ)**
*"Moreover He will bring back on you all the diseases of Egypt, of which you were afraid, and they shall cling to you."*

**Verse 60 (Literal Hebrew)**
*"The Lord will permit you to suffer all the sickness and diseases the Egyptians have suffered."*

(17) All the diseases of Egypt refers to all kinds of sickness and any type of disease.

**For example, all the diseases of Egypt would include:**
- Hay fever
- Strokes (rupture of a blood vessel in the brain causing paralysis)

# God's Healing Power

- Heart problems
- Sinus problems
- Sore throat
- Deafness
- Migraine headaches
- Kidney/Liver disease
- Thyroid condition
- Glandular problems

- Mumps
- Measles
- All types of allergies
- Sugar diabetes
- High blood pressure
- Back problems
- Physical deformities
- Blood disease/leukemia

## Verse 61 (NKJ)
*"Also every sickness and every plague, which is not written in the book of the law, will the Lord bring upon you until you are destroyed.*

## Verse 61 (Literal Hebrew)
*"And that is not all because the Lord will allow you to be afflicted with every type of sickness and any kind of disease He has not listed in His Word until you are destroyed."*

(18) Every sickness and every disease not specified in God's Word. That includes all new virus infections, all kinds of cancer, AIDS, all incurable diseases, etc. It covers your case.

## Verse 65, 66 (NKJ)
*"...but there the Lord will give you a trembling heart, failing eyes, and anguish of soul. Your life shall hang in doubt before you; you shall fear day and night, and have no assurance of life."*

## Verses 65, 66 (Literal Hebrew)
*"The Lord will permit you to have heart problems and bad eyesight, He will let you walk around oppressed by fear night and day."*

(19) Trembling heart - heart problems caused by anxiety and fear.

(20) Failing eyes - All types of eye complaints e.g. bad eyesight, cataracts, etc.

# God's Healing Power

**PERSONAL NOTES**

## A SUMMARY OF THE CURSE OF SICKNESS IN DEUTERONOMY 28

THE CURSE OF SICKNESS INCLUDES:

(1) Epidemics such as the flu

(2) Deadly diseases such as AIDS

(3) T.B., bronchitis, and asthma

(4) All types of fever

(5) Ulcers

(6) Cancer

(7) Malaria

(8) Jaundice

(9) All sexually transmitted diseases

(10) Tumors and malignant growths, lumps in your body

(11) Hemorrhoids

(12) Acne, eczema, and all skin diseases

(13) Mental oppression, depression and confusion in the mind

(14) Bad eyesight, cataracts, blindness

(15) Nervous tension and nervous breakdown

(16) Arthritis and rheumatism

(17) Bone disease and physical deformities

(18) Boils all over the body, back problems

(19) Incurable diseases

(20) Chronic sicknesses that last for years

(21) Heart problems

(22) All the diseases of Egypt (All known and unknown diseases in the world today)

(23) Every sickness not mentioned in the Bible

(24) Every disease not listed in God's Word

## DOMINION OVER DISEASE

The Good News of the Gospel is that Christ has already delivered, redeemed, and set us free from every curse of sickness at the cross. Healing and health is our portion, not sickness and disease.

Matthew 8:16, 17    Galatians 3:13, 14    1 Peter 2:24    Romans 8:2

# God's Healing Power

### E. W. Kenyon:

"When we recognize the fact that our sickness was laid on Christ, and that He bore our diseases in His body on the tree, and that by His stripes we are healed, it will be the end of the dominion of disease in our lives. Sin and disease have been put away, and in the Name of Jesus we have dominion over Satan and the work of his hands. In the Name of Jesus we cast out demons, we can also lay hands on the sick and they do recover. If we can cast out demons, we can also command the demon disease to leave our bodies, for disease was brought there by a demon and is being developed by a demon. We say, 'In Jesus' Name, demon, leave this body.' That demon is under obligation to the Name of Jesus to obey."

*"Or do you not know that your body is the temple of the Holy Spirit who is in you, whom you have from God, and you are not your own? For you were bought with a price; therefore glorify God in your body and in your spirit, which are God's."*

1 Corinthians 6:19, 20

The body of the Christian is God's property, not the devil's dumping ground. In the name of Jesus we have victory and dominion over disease.

The Holy Spirit indwells and lives inside the body of the believer. Your body belongs to the Holy Spirit, NOT demon spirits.

A healthy body glorifies God, NOT a sick, diseased body.

## WHAT ARE THE BIBLE FACTS ABOUT DIVINE HEALING?

The Bible says that your body is the Lord's.

1 Corinthians 6:13

The Bible says that your body belongs to God, not to the devil or sickness.

1 Corinthians 6:19, 20

The Bible says that Jesus is the Savior of your body.

Ephesians 5:23

Healing and health is the will of God for your body not sickness and disease.

3 John 2

Healing for the physical body and the forgiveness of sins are inseparable; they always go together. They are the Siamese twins of the Gospel.

*"Who forgives all your iniquities, Who heals all your diseases."*

Psalm 103:3

# God's Healing Power

© 1994 The Believer's School of Training, Rev. Norman K. Robertson

**PERSONAL NOTES**

*"Which is easier, to say to the paralytic, 'Your sins are forgiven you,' or to say, 'Arise, take up your bed and walk'?"*

**Mark 2:9**

Job 42: 10 (AMP) – God, the Father calls all sickness **CAPTIVITY**.

Luke 13:16 – Jesus calls sickness and disease **SATANIC BONDAGE**.

Acts 10:38 – The Holy Spirit calls all sickness **OPPRESSION OF THE DEVIL**.

Deuteronomy 28:15-68 – Calls all sickness **A CURSE**.

As far as God and the Bible are concerned, all sickness, all disease, all physical infirmity and affliction are CAPTIVITY, SATANIC BONDAGE, OPPRESSION OF THE DEVIL – A CURSE.

Disease = Broken ease, "Dis-ease."

Sickness = Death in operation.

"Sickness and disease is the foul offspring of its mother, Sin and its father, Satan."

John Alexander Dowie

*"Therefore if the Son makes you free, you shall be free indeed."*

**John 8:36**

Jesus came to release us, redeem us, and set us free from the bondage of sickness.

**FACT 1**    The attributes, nature, and character of God are against all sickness and disease.
Genesis 1:31
Exodus 23:25, 26
3 John 2

**FACT 2**    Deliverance from all sickness and all disease was paid for by Christ on the cross.
1 Peter 2:24
Matthew 8:16, 17
Galatians 3:13, 14

**FACT 3**    The Lord Jesus Christ gave every Christian dominion over all sickness and all disease.
Luke 9:1, 2
Luke 10:17-19
James 4:7

**FACT 4**    The power of the name of Jesus and the anointing of the Holy Spirit destroys the yoke of all sickness.
Isaiah 10:27
Acts 10:38
Philippians 2:9-11

**FACT 5**    The will of God for every person is healing, health, and long life.
Matthew 4:23, 24 (Healing)
Proverbs 4:20-22 (Health)
Job 5:26 (Long Life)

# God's Healing Power

Notice in Matthew 4:23, 24 Jesus, who is still the same today, healed all sickness, all disease, and all sick people.

That INCLUDES all sick people – EVERYBODY.

It INCLUDES all sicknesses – EVERYTHING.

## BIBLE WAYS TO RECEIVE YOUR HEALING

**(1) You can receive healing through the MEDICINE OF GOD'S WORD.**

**Proverbs 4:20-22**

Repeated listening to God's Healing Scriptures, meditating on and confession with your mouth will bring healing and health to your body.

Receive the Word of God with focused attention through the EAR GATE, the EYE GATE, and with your MIND.

**Psalm 107:19, 20**

Notice:    The Word of God **saves us, heals us**, and **delivers us**.

The medicine of God's Word will heal you and keep you healthy.

**(2) You can receive healing through the LAYING ON OF HANDS.**

**Mark 16:17, 18, 20**

According to Romans 1:16, God's Word is dynamic and powerful. When we preach, teach, and minister God's Word, the Holy Spirit CONFIRMS the Word with supernatural healing. The laying on of hands in obedience to the great commission transmits God's healing power into the sick to drive out disease and effect a healing cure.

**(3) You can receive healing through the PRAYER OF FAITH AND ANOINTING WITH OIL.**

**James 5:14, 15**

Christians stay sick because they never call for the Elders of the Church. We must OPERATE in obedience to God's Word. We must do what God says to do.

**The foundation for our physical healing is that it is through Christ – by the Holy Spirit – according to the Word of God.**

**(4) You can receive healing through SPIRITUAL GIFTS.**

**1 Corinthians 12:9, 10, 28**

Miracles and gifts of healings are placed by God in the church and no man has ever had any right or authority to take them out of the church.

Healing is the provision of God because it is the children's bread.

# God's Healing Power

© 1994 The Believer's School of Training, Rev. Norman K. Robertson

**PERSONAL NOTES**

## STAYING IN HEALTH

(1) Continually living in physical health (not getting sick) is God's will for every believer.

**3 John 2**

The will of God for the Christian is not to keep getting sick and keep getting healed. The will of God is for you to stay well.

(2) Health and remaining healthy is a decision you make.

**Deuteronomy 30:11-20**

Being passive and not putting the Word into ACTION in your life will produce death in your life.

**Romans 10:8-10**

You make your decision with your HEART and confess your decision with your MOUTH. Take the Bible and boldly declare the healing Scriptures ...

IT IS WRITTEN:

- Exodus 15:26
- Matthew 8:16, 17
- Psalm 103:3
- Jeremiah 33:6
- 1 Peter 2:24
- 3 John 2

## THE IMPORTANCE OF SPEAKING GOD'S WORD

Confession of the Word is vital. Your words are very important. They can carry:

- Faith or Fear
- Healing or Sickness
- Blessing or Cursing
- Victory or Defeat

We need to start confessing what God's Word says.

Right confession gives your spirit man lordship over your mind and over your body.

*"You are snared by the words of your mouth."*   **Proverbs 6:2**

Your words dominate you, control you, ensnare you.

Confessing God's promises is agreeing with God out loud.

# God's Healing Power

<u>Why Confess?</u>

*"Therefore, holy brethren, partakers of the heavenly calling, consider the Apostle and High Priest of our confession, Christ Jesus."*
Hebrews 3:1

*"Seeing then that we have a great High Priest who has passed through the heavens, Jesus the Son of God, let us hold fast our confession."*
Hebrews 4:14

*"Let us hold fast the confession of our hope without wavering, for He who promised is faithful."*
Hebrews 10:23

<u>Christianity is called The Great Confession.</u>

*"But what does it say? 'The word is near you, in your mouth and in your heart' (that is, the word of faith which we preach)."*
Romans 10:8

*"That if you confess with your mouth the Lord Jesus and believe in your heart that God has raised Him from the dead, you will be saved. For with the heart one believes unto righteousness, and with the mouth confession is made unto salvation."*
Romans 10:9, 10

<u>With the mouth confession is made unto SALVATION. ("SOZO").</u>

Salvation is more than spiritual. It is also physical – physical healing for the body.

Confession can bring salvation to my spirit and confession can bring healing to my body.

*"...these things I want you to affirm constantly, that those who have believed in God should be careful to maintain good works. These things are good and profitable to men."*
Titus 3:8

<u>We are to AFFIRM CONSTANTLY the Word of God.</u>

*"That the communication of thy faith may become effectual by the acknowledging of every good thing which is in you in Christ Jesus."*
Philemon 6 (KJV)

<u>We are to ACKNOWLEDGE our faith constantly.</u>

*"Whoso offereth praise glorifieth me: and to him that ordereth his conversation aright will I shew the salvation of God."*
Psalm 50:23 (KJV)

# God's Healing Power

**PERSONAL NOTES**

Your conversation must be in agreement with God's Word.

*"Your words have been harsh against Me," Says the Lord, 'Yet you say, 'What have we spoken against you'?"*

**Malachi 3:13**

Your wrong confession, your negative conversation, put you in opposition with God Almighty.

*"He who guards his mouth and his tongue keeps himself from troubles."*

**Proverbs 21:23 (AMP)**

Watch your mouth or else it will get you into trouble.

Right CONFESSION brings healing to your body.

*"Put Me in remembrance; Let us contend together; State your case, that you may be acquitted."*

**Isaiah 43:26**

God says, "Put me in remembrance of MY WORDS."

God tells us to remind Him of His promises.

The Bible says:

    We are to remind God of what He has said.

    We are to remind God of His Covenant.

    We are to remind God of His Promises.

    Keep on repeating, speaking, and reminding God of what His Bible says.

*"Therefore, holy brethren, partakers of the heavenly calling, consider the Apostle and High Priest of our confession, Christ Jesus."*

**Hebrews 3:1**

Notice that Scripture says **Jesus is the HIGH PRIEST of what I confess.**

CONFESS:

    Jesus, you are my Healer.

    Jesus, by your stripes I am well.

**Jesus says what you say, and the Holy Spirit enforces it in your body.**

- What I confess, Jesus will confess.

- **Jesus is the Great High Priest of my confession.**

- What I confess, speak, declare, and boldly proclaim, Jesus speaks in Heaven before the Father, and the Holy Spirit activates and makes a reality in my life on earth.

**IMPORTANT:** *Take 15 minutes each day and meditate upon these powerful Divine Healing Truths until they become established in your heart.*

**PERSONAL NOTES**

## KEY QUESTIONS

(1) What is divine healing?

(2) What Scriptures reveal God's covenant of healing?

(3) What are the seven redemptive covenant names of God?

(4) At the cross, did Jesus redeem us from all sickness? Explain what He did and what He took for us.

(5) Give six reasons why Satan is the author of sickness.

(6) If Isaiah 53:5 states, "By His stripes you **are** healed," why does 1 Peter 2:24, "By His stripes you **were** healed"?

## MEMORY WORK

Exodus 23:25, 26

Acts 10:38

1 Peter 2:24

## PERSONAL APPLICATION

(1) Explain why you believe it is God's will for you to be healed.

(2) Do you have a personal testimony of God's healing power in your life?

(3) If someone was sick and needed ministry, how would you share the Bible message of divine healing with him or her?

(4) Do you look for opportunities to pray for sick people? If not will you start today?

(5) Do you know how to walk in the reality of God's Word, resist sickness, and stay healthy?

## RECOMMENDED READING

T. L. Osborn, *Healing the Sick*

E. W. Kenyon, *Jesus the Healer*

Kenneth E. Hagin, *Redeemed*

# LESSON: 7                                         Christ The Healer

**KEY VERSE:**     Acts 10:38     *"How God anointed Jesus of Nazareth with the Holy Spirit and with power, who went about doing good and healing all who were oppressed by the devil, for God was with Him."*

**KEY TRUTH:**     The foundation for our healing is that it is through Christ, by the Holy Spirit according to the Word of God.

A lack of assurance or a lack of knowledge concerning the will of God to heal you is a blockage to receiving your healing. So often, people are plagued with all kinds of doubts and questions when it comes to receiving physical healing.

- Is it God's will to heal all?
- Is it God's will to heal only some?
- Is sickness sometimes the will of God?

FAITH BEGINS WHERE THE WILL OF GOD IS KNOWN.

The will of God is revealed in the pages of the Word of God.

Scripture is the source that reveals the will of God.

## GOD'S WILL CONCERNING HEALING

(1) The Word of God reveals that healing is the will of God because it is the nature of God to heal. In Exodus 15:26, God says, "I am your Healer – Doctor – Physician."

The nature of God is against all sickness and disease. Healing is the nature of God.

(2) God's will concerning healing is revealed through the ministry of Jesus.
                                        **Acts 10:38**

(3) Healing is the will of God because it has already been provided through the cross of Jesus.
                                        **1 Peter 2:24**

God revealed Himself as the Healer, the Doctor, and the Great Physician of His covenant people in the Old Testament.

God said, "I am your Doctor – your Physician – Your Healer."

Exodus 15:26 declares, "I am the Lord Your Healer."

Malachi 3:6 declares, "I am the Lord, I do not change."

Hebrews 13:8 declares, "Jesus Christ the same yesterday, today, and forever."

# Christ The Healer

© 1994 The Believer's School of Training, Rev. Norman K. Robertson

**PERSONAL NOTES**

GOD AND HIS NATURE ARE UNCHANGING.

*"Every good gift and every perfect gift is from above, and comes down from the Father of lights, with whom there is no variation or shadow of turning."*

**James 1:17**

God is good and He only gives good gifts. He never changes. His nature never changes.

God's will concerning healing was clearly revealed in the ministry of Jesus.

*"How God anointed Jesus of Nazareth with the Holy Spirit and with power, who went about doing good and healing all who were oppressed by the devil, for God was with Him."*

**Acts 10:38**

The Trinity – Father, Son, and Holy Spirit – are united and together in agreement in the ministry of healing.

- Healing is from God; sickness is from the devil.

- The Trinity – Father, Son and Holy Spirit – are united in bringing healing to suffering humanity.

- The devil brings sickness. God brings healing.

*"For I have come down from heaven, not to do My own will, but the will of Him who sent Me."*

**John 6:38**

*"Jesus said to him, 'Have I been with you so long, and yet you have not known me, Philip?' He who has seen Me has seen the Father; so how can you say, 'Show us the Father'?"*

**John 14:9**

## THE MIRACLE MINISTRY OF JESUS CHRIST
## SEVENTEEN MIRACLES OF HEALING

(1)  Nobleman's Son - John 4:46-54, Capernaum.

(2)  Infirm Man - John 5:1-9, Jerusalem.

(3)  Peter's Mother-in-law - Matthew 8:14-17; Mark 1:29-31; Luke 4:38-39, Capernaum.

(4)  A Leper - Matthew 8:2-4; Mark 1:40-45; Luke 5:12-15.

(5)  A Paralytic - Matthew 9:2-8; Mark 2:3-12; Luke 5:17-26, Capernaum.

(6)  Man with Withered Hand - Matthew 12:9-14; Mark 3:1-6; Luke 6:6-11.

(7)  Centurion's Servant - Matthew 8:5-13; Luke 7:1-10, Capernaum.

(8)  Two Blind Men - Matthew 9:27-31, Capernaum.

(9)  Deaf and Dumb Man - Mark 7:31-37, Decapolis.

# Christ The Healer

(10) Blind Man at Bethsaida - Mark 8:22-26

(11) Blind Man in Jerusalem - John 9:1-12

(12) Woman of 18 Years' Infirmity - Luke 13:10-17, Galilee.

(13) Woman with Hemorrhage - Matthew 9:20-22; Mark 5:25-34; Luke 8:43-48, Capernaum.

(14) Man with Dropsy - Luke 14:1-6.

(15) Ten Lepers - Luke 17:11-19, Borders of Samaria.

(16) Blind Bartimaeus - Matthew 20:29-34; Mark 10:46-52; Luke 18:35-43, Jericho.

(17) Malchus' Ear Restored - Luke 22:50-51, Gethsemane.

## SEVEN MIRACLES OF CASTING OUT DEMONS

(1) A Demoniac in the Synagogue - Mark 1:21-28; Luke 4:31-37, Capernaum.

(2) A Blind and Dumb Demoniac - Matthew 12:22; Luke 11:14, Capernaum.

(3) Gedarene Demoniacs - Matthew 8:28-34; Mark 5:1-20; Luke 8:26-39, Gadara.

(4) A Dumb Demoniac - Matthew 9:32-34.

(5) The Syrophoenician's Daughter - Matthew 15:21-28, Mark 7:24-30, Tyre.

(6) The Epileptic Boy - Matthew 17:14-21; Mark 9:14-29; Luke 9:37-43, Mt. Hermon.

(7) Mary Magdalene - Luke 8:2.

The person and ministry of Jesus demonstrated the will of God concerning healing. Carefully read through the four Gospels and examine the healing ministry of Jesus and you will discover the following facts:

- Jesus never once refused to heal anyone who came to Him for healing.

- ALL who came to Jesus for healing were healed.

- Jesus never once said to any sick person:

    "It is not the will of God to heal you."

    "Your sickness is a thorn in the flesh."

    "There is a reason for your sickness. It is for the glory of God."

    "God, if it is your will, heal this person."

    "Your sickness is incurable. I can't help you."

    "God is making you a better person through this trial of sickness."

- Those who did not come to Jesus did not get healed. Jesus never turned anyone away who was sick and came to Him for healing.

The Bible tells us specifically the kinds of sickness that we have been delivered from. Study carefully the List of Curses in Deuteronomy 28:15-68.

# Christ The Healer

© 1994 The Believer's School of Training, Rev. Norman K. Robertson

## JESUS THE WILL OF GOD IN ACTION

Every single person in Bible days who was sick and came to Jesus for healing was healed.

When you see Jesus in His healing ministry, you see God the Father in action.

* Father, Son, and Holy Spirit are united together in bringing healing to sick and suffering humanity.

**Acts 10:38**

* The will of God concerning healing was demonstrated in the person and ministry of Jesus.

**Hebrews 13:8**
**Matthew 4:23, 24**

* Physical healing belongs to us today because at the cross two thousand years ago, Jesus took upon Himself all our pains, sicknesses, and disease.

**Isaiah 53:4, 5**
**Matthew 8:16, 17**
**1 Peter 2:24**

* Deliverance from all sickness, all pains, and all disease was obtained for us by Jesus on the cross.

**Galatians 3:13**

*"Jesus Christ is the same yesterday, today and forever."*

**Hebrews 13:8**

The Jesus of Bible days is the exact same Jesus today as He was back then.

In Bible days:

* Did Jesus heal sick people?  Yes!
* Did Jesus cast out demons and set people free?  Yes!
* Is Jesus part of the Godhead?  Yes!
* Was Jesus the visible manifestation of the Father on earth?  Yes!

God is the God of the now. He said, "I am!"

God is a God of the present tense.

*"Jesus is the same identical person in every respect TODAY as He was YESTER-DAY and He will be the exact same TOMORROW."*

**Hebrews 13:8**
**(Greek New Testament)**

# Christ The Healer

*"He is the sole expression of the glory of God the Light-being, the out-raying of the divine and He is the perfect imprint and very image of [God's] nature..."*

Hebrews 1:3 (AMP)

Jesus walked this earth as the perfect expression of God's nature and God's will to man. Jesus said, "If you have seen me then you have seen the Father."

- Jesus came to show us the will of God.
- Jesus was the will of God in ACTION.

*"I can of Myself do nothing. As I hear, I judge; and My judgment is righteous, because I do not seek My own will but the will of the Father who sent Me."*

John 5:30

*"For I have come down from heaven, not to do My own will, but the will of Him who sent Me."*

John 6:38

*"And He who sent Me is with Me. The Father has not left Me alone, for I always do those things that please Him."*

John 8:29

*"And He who sees Me sees Him who sent Me. I have come as a light into the world, that whoever believes in Me should not abide in darkness."*

John 12:45, 46

*"And Jesus went about all Galilee, teaching in their synagogues, preaching the gospel of the kingdom, and healing all kinds of sickness and all kinds of disease among the people. Then His fame went throughout all Syria; and they brought to Him all sick people who were afflicted with various diseases and torments, and those who were demon-possessed, epileptics, and paralytics; and He healed them."*

Matthew 4:23, 24

*"When evening had come, they brought to Him many who were demon-possessed. And He cast out the spirits with a word, and healed all who were sick, that it might be fulfilled which was spoken by Isaiah the prophet saying: 'He Himself took our infirmities and bore our sicknesses.'"*

Matthew 8:16, 17

*"Then Jesus went about all the cities and villages, teaching in their synagogues, preaching the gospel of the kingdom, and healing every sickness and every disease among the people."*

Matthew 9:35

# Christ The Healer

**PERSONAL NOTES**

*"And when He had called His twelve disciples to Him, He gave them power over unclean spirits, to cast them out, and to heal all kinds of sickness and all kinds of disease."*

**Matthew 10:1**

*"But when Jesus knew it, He withdrew from there. And great multitudes followed Him, and He healed them all."*

**Matthew 12:15**

*"And when Jesus went out He saw a great multitude; and He was moved with compassion for them, and healed their sick."*

**Matthew 14:14**

*"When the sun was setting, all those who had any that were sick with various diseases brought them to Him; and He laid His hands on every one of them and healed them."*

**Luke 4:40**

*"And He came down with them and stood on a level place with a crowd of His disciples and a great multitude of people from all Judea and Jerusalem, and from the sea-coast of Tyre and Sidon, who came to hear Him and be healed of their diseases, as well as those who were tormented with unclean spirits. And they were healed. And the whole multitude sought to touch Him, for power went out from Him and healed them all."*

**Luke 6:17-19**

## HOW JESUS HEALED IN BIBLE DAYS

(1) Jesus healed all kinds of sickness, all types of disease, and all sick people.
**Matthew 4:23, 24**

(2) Jesus healed all who were sick and cast out demon spirits of infirmity responsible for the sickness.

**Matthew 8:16**

(3) The method of Jesus was teaching God's Word, preaching the Gospel, then healing the sick. He healed every sickness and every disease.

**Matthew 9:35**

(4) Jesus gave His disciples power to heal all kinds of sickness and all kinds of disease.
**Matthew 10:1**
**Luke 9:1, 2**

(5) In Matthew 12:15 Jesus healed all who were sick.

(6) In Matthew 14:14 Jesus, because of compassion, healed all sick people in a great multitude.

**PERSONAL NOTES**

(7) In Matthew 14:34-36 every sick person and every diseased person who touched Jesus was healed.

(8) In Luke 4:38-40 and Luke 9:11 we see that Jesus healed everybody who needed healing.

(9) In Luke 4:40 every sick person Jesus laid His hands upon was healed.

(10) *"How God anointed Jesus of Nazareth with the Holy Spirit and with power, who went about doing good and healing all who were oppressed by the devil, for God was with Him."*

Acts 10:38

## NOTICE:

(1) Everybody that Jesus healed was Satanically oppressed.

(2) Jesus healed all – not 50%, not 7 out of 10, but ALL.

Sickness is Satanic oppression. Christ is the Healer and Satan is the oppressor.

Luke 13:10-16

## NOTICE:

(1) This woman had a spirit of infirmity for 18 years. Sickness can be caused by a demon of infirmity.                    Luke 13:11

(2) Satan had bound her with this affliction.

Sickness is the bondage of Satan.                    Luke 13:16

(3) She was a daughter of the covenant and had the right to be free. Jesus healed her and set her free. He did not leave her sick.

Luke 13:16

Jesus came to earth as the perfect expression of the will of God for mankind.

Jesus clearly demonstrated by His words and His works what the will of God was – deliverance from sickness.

In the ministry of Jesus we see that the nature of God is against disease and it is the nature of God to heal.

Healing is the nature of God.

The knowledge of God's will concerning sickness and healing is clearly revealed in the ministry of Jesus.

- He only did the Father's will.

- He only spoke the Father's words.

- He only did the Father's works.

# Christ The Healer

**PERSONAL NOTES**

In Bible Days:

- Jesus healed all who came to Him.
- Jesus did not turn anyone down.
- Jesus never told any person:

  "Your sickness is for God's glory."

  "Your sickness is a test of faith."

  "Your sickness is the will of God."

  "Your sickness is making you a better person."

  "Your sickness is a blessing."

  "Your sickness is a thorn in the flesh sent by God."

- Jesus NEVER refused to heal anybody.
- Jesus came to destroy the works of the devil.
- Jesus healed all He laid His hands upon.

*"Then great multitudes came to Him, having with them the lame, blind, mute, maimed, and many others; and they laid them down at Jesus' feet, and He healed them. So the multitude marvelled when they saw the mute speaking, the maimed made whole, the lame walking, and the blind seeing; and they glorified the God of Israel."*

Matthew 15:30, 31

*"Jesus Christ is the same yesterday, today, and forever."*

Hebrews 13:8

Today, healing from every disease is available for every person who will come to Jesus in faith.

## THE COMPASSION OF OUR LORD

Back in Bible days, many times when the sick came seeking healing they asked for mercy (compassion). They approached the Lord for healing, calling upon His mercy. For example, blind Bartimaeus.

**F. F. BOSWORTH said,** "The most conspicuous statements in the Scriptures about our Heavenly Father are the declarations of His love, His mercy, and His compassion."

*"The Lord is gracious and full of compassion, Slow to anger and great in mercy. The Lord is good to all, And His tender mercies are over all His works."*

Psalm 145:8, 9

# Christ The Healer

Once people catch the revelation of God's love and compassion towards them, their days of sickness will be over.

When Jesus healed the sick, He unveiled and showed the compassionate heart of God. That is why the multitudes came to Him.

Jesus, by healing the sick in His compassion, was expressing the compassionate heart of God to the people.

The compassion of God towards the sick was a revelation of the will of God.

As we go through the four Gospels and look carefully at the ministry of our Lord Jesus Christ, we see in a number of places how Jesus was moved with compassion for those who were sick and had need of healing.

It was because of His compassion that He healed, and today Jesus is still the same. He has not changed. According to Hebrews 13:8 Jesus is unchangeable. He is the SAME (including His compassion for the sick) yesterday, today, and forever!

Jesus healed the sick because of His compassion.

The Bible repeatedly states that Jesus was moved with compassion and healed those who were sick.

Compassion was the motivating, driving force that compelled Jesus to heal the people.

Jesus did not heal the sick to prove His deity.

Jesus did not heal sick people to promote Himself or His ministry.

Jesus did not heal people to prove He was God.

Healing the sick is a revelation of God's mercy.

Healing the sick is an expression of God's heart of compassion.

Jesus' mercy is no different and no less than it was back in Bible days.

## COMPASSION AND MERCY

Compassion "FEELS" the need and mercy "FILLS" the need.

Mercy defined: It is kindness that gives help to the most undeserving.

Compassion defined: It is the compelling desire to bear and relieve another's distress and suffering.

*"However, the report went around concerning Him all the more; and great multitudes came together to hear, and to be healed by Him of their infirmities."*

**Luke 5:15**

**NOTICE:** Great multitudes came to hear and to be healed. Healing follows hearing.

God is not a respecter of persons when it comes to bestowing His mercies upon people in need.

The benevolent heart of God reaches out to all of mankind. That is the reason for Calvary.

# Christ The Healer

It was compassion that moved Jesus to heal the sick and suffering in Bible days and Jesus has not changed.

**Hebrews 13:8**

(1) **THE HEALING OF THE LEPER** was a display of God's compassion.
Verse 41: "and Jesus MOVED with compassion."

**Mark 1:40-42**

(2) **THE HEALING OF THE MULTITUDES** revealed the compassion and mercy of our Father God.

**Matthew 14:13, 14**

Notice in verse 14, the compassion of Jesus produced healing for the sick.

(3) **THE HEALING OF TWO BLIND MEN** came as a result of God's mercy and compassion.

**Matthew 20:29-34**

The two blind men desiring healing asked for mercy.

Healing is a mercy.

God is merciful. He is full of mercy. He is full of compassion.

*"Blessed be the God and Father of our Lord Jesus Christ, the Father of mercies and God of all comfort."*

**2 Corinthians 1:3**

(4) **GOD IS THE FATHER OF MERCIES.** That is one of God's names.

The sick in Bible days asked for mercy and they received healing.

*"But when the multitudes knew it, they followed Him; and He received them and spoke to them about the kingdom of God, and healed those who had need of healing."*

**Luke 9:11**

Jesus healed the sick because of His love, His mercy and His compassion toward them.

(5) **THE DEMON-POSSESSED MAN OF GADARA WAS SUPERNATURALLY DELIVERED** and set free from demon powers because of the Lord's compassion.

*"However, Jesus did not permit him, but said to him, 'Go home to your friends, and tell them what great things the Lord has done for you, and how He has had compassion on you.'"*

**Mark 5:19**

Notice how the Lord has had "compassion" on you.

The Lord's compassion, mercy, and love was the compelling force that delivered Legion from demonic possession of 6,000 evil spirits. (Legion = 6,000)

Jesus instructed this man after his deliverance to GO and TELL (SHARE, TESTIFY,

# Christ The Healer

PROCLAIM) his family, friends, and the people in Decapolis, where he came from, the great things the Lord had done for him, especially God's compassion.

*"And he departed and began to proclaim in Decapolis all that Jesus had done for him; and all marveled."*

Mark 5:20

In Matthew 15:30, 31, we see the results of the delivered man's testimony in Decapolis.

*"Then great multitudes came to Him, having with them the lame, blind, mute, maimed, and many others; and they laid them down at Jesus' feet, and He healed them. So the multitude marveled when they saw the mute speaking, the maimed made whole, the lame walking, and the blind seeing; and they glorified the God of Israel."*

Matthew 15:30, 31

It is important that we testify and go and tell others when God heals our bodies, answers our prayers, and blesses us.

Matthew 9:35-10:1

God's compassion is God's divine love in action.

*"Most assuredly, I say to you, he who believes in Me, the works that I do he will do also; and greater works than these he will do, because I go to My Father."*

John 14:12

Jesus taught and emphasized that His disciples, His church, and every believer today should be carriers of the mercy of God.

The healing miracles of Jesus were a display of God's compassion.

Christ's compassion towards the sick has never changed.

*"The blind see and the lame walk; the lepers are cleansed and the deaf hear; the dead are raised up and the poor have the gospel preached to them."*

Matthew 11:5

Jesus' works of compassion are the same today – the unchanging healing ministry of Christ is based on His unchangeable compassion.

**F. F. Bosworth said,** "The Age of Miracles and Gifts of Healing has not passed away because Jesus has NEVER WITHDRAWN His compassion or mercies towards needy humanity."

*"Bless the Lord, O my soul, and forget not all His benefits: Who forgives all your iniquities, Who heals all your diseases."*

Psalm 103:2, 3

The mercy of healing is available for us just as much as the mercy of forgiveness of sins.

# Christ The Healer

## CHRIST REDEEMED US FROM SICKNESS

| | |
|---|---|
| (1) Jesus has "redeemed" us from spiritual death. | **Romans 5:12-19** |
| (2) Jesus has "redeemed" us from the curse of poverty. | **2 Corinthians 8:9** |
| (3) Jesus has "redeemed" us from the curse of sickness and disease. | **Galatians 3:13, 14** |

*"For the law of the Spirit of life in Christ Jesus has made me free from the law of sin and death."*

**Romans 8:2**

*"Christ has redeemed us from the curse of the law, having become a curse for us (for it is written, 'Cursed is everyone who hangs on a tree')."*

**Galatians 3:13**

*"Who Himself bore our sins in His own body on the tree, that we, having died to sins, might live for righteousness – by whose stripes you were healed."*

**1 Peter 2:24**

## WHAT CATEGORIES OF SICKNESSES HAS JESUS REDEEMED US FROM?

The curse of sickness is listed in Deuteronomy, Chapter 28.

Read carefully Deuteronomy 28:15, 21, 22, 27-29, 35, 58-61, 65.

• What are the specific sicknesses mentioned in the Bible?

**DEUTERONOMY CHAPTER 28**

| | |
|---|---|
| **(1) Pestilence/the plague** | **v. 21** - any kind of epidemic or deadly disease – AIDS. |
| **(2) Consumption** | **v. 22** - tuberculosis, bronchitis, lung infections, wasting disease. |
| **(3) Fever** | **v. 22** - all types of fever e.g., hay fever, typhoid, yellow, scarlet. |
| **(4) Inflammation** | **v. 22** - refers to all types of cancer. |
| **(5) Severe burning fever** | **v. 22** - malaria, sunstroke, tropical diseases. |
| **(6) Botch of Egypt/Boils** | **v. 27** - ulcers, boils, all sexually transmitted diseases. |
| **(7) Emerods/Tumors** | **v. 27** - refers to growths, lumps, cysts, warts, hemorrhoids, all types of tumors. |
| **(8) Scab** | **v. 27** - refers to scurvy, scalp and skin eczema, dermatitis, acne. |
| **(9) Itch** | **v. 27** - refers to all kinds of skin complaints and skin diseases. |

# Christ The Healer

**(10) Madness**  — v. 28 - insanity, mental disorders, all mental oppression, mental breakdown.

**(11) Blindness**  — v. 28 - eye problems leading to loss of sight, cataracts glaucoma, etc.

**(12) Confusion of Heart**  — v. 28 - confusion of the mind, dismay, fear, anxiety, deep depression, attacks on the nerves and nervous breakdown.

**(13) Problems with the knees and legs**  — v. 35 - stiffness and pain in the joints, rheumatism, arthritis, etc.

**(14) Boils/sores which cannot be healed**  — v. 35 - all types of boils and sores.

**(15) Prolonged sicknesses/ sicknesses of long continuance**  — v. 59 - chronic illnesses, recurring health problems, e.g. migraine headaches, sinus problems, asthma, arthritis, heart problems, incurable diseases, any type of recurring or long-lasting sickness.

**(16) All the diseases of Egypt**  — v. 60 - every type of sickness and illness known in the world, listed by the medical profession including AIDS.

**(17) Every sickness and every disease not mentioned**  — v. 61 - those not known by medical profession or not listed in a medical dictionary.

**(18) A trembling heart and failing eyes**  — v. 65 - any type of heart condition and eye problem, bad eye sight.

**Your case, whatever your illness or condition, is covered by the Bible and the cross of Jesus.**

Pay attention to the plain, clear teaching of Scripture. Listen to God's Word. It is very clear. Sickness and disease are thieves and robbers – curses rather than blessings. Sickness and disease are enemies. The cross of Jesus covers every condition in your body.

Sickness and disease are not the will of God for His children. God does not want you living under the curse, but under the blessing!

The only time Jesus was ever sick was when He took your sickness at Calvary.

# Christt The Healer

**PERSONAL NOTES**

All pain, sickness, and every kind of disease was placed on Jesus at the cross.

This includes:

HEADACHES, MIGRAINES,

BACKACHES, BACK PROBLEMS,

ALL CANCER, TUMORS,

HEART DISEASE, BLOOD DISEASE,

ARTHRITIS, RHEUMATISM,

ASTHMA, BRONCHITIS, PNEUMONIA,

DEAFNESS, BLINDNESS,

LIVER DISEASE, DIABETES,

ALL ACHES AND PAINS,

CATARACTS, HIGH BLOOD PRESSURE,

STOMACH AND INTESTINAL DISORDERS,

THYROID CONDITION,

BONE CANCER,

AIDS, PLUS EVERY OTHER DISEASE AND AILMENT AFFLICTING HUMANITY.

This also includes "soulish afflictions" such as fear, anxiety, tension, and depression — even sleeplessness.

Jesus took all these upon Himself and carried them away!

All your sickness was laid upon Jesus so you can be healed and healthy.

If you can believe the Blood of Jesus Christ washed your sins away and paid for your salvation, then believe the same Blood obtained physical healing for your body.

**Matthew 8:16, 17**
**1 Peter 2:24**

Physical healing and physical well-being is in the cross.

The Blood of Jesus removed and washed your sins away, and the same Blood of Jesus provided physical healing for your body.

There is healing in the Blood of Jesus to give you freedom from all pains, all sicknesses, and all diseases.

Your attitude towards healing will determine God's response toward healing your body. There can be no room for doubt or unbelief.

- Healing is God's nature and character.
- Healing is in God's name – Jehovah Rapha (name of Jesus).
- Healing is in God's Word.
- Healing is in the cross. It is our blood right.

# Christ The Healer

**PERSONAL NOTES**

## THE ABC'S OF HEALING

(1) **It is God's will to heal you personally** — not just somebody else.

                                               3 John 2

(2) **All sickness and all disease is the work of Satan.**     Acts 10:38

(3) **God calls all sickness:**

     **A CURSE**                                      Galatians 3:13

     **SATANIC BONDAGE**                   Luke 13:10-16

     **THE OPPRESSION OF THE DEVIL**       Acts 10:38

Today, every "Daughter" of Abraham (Blood Covenant Child of God) should be healed and free from sickness.

(4) **Healing is God's will because God was a Healer in the Old Testament and He is the Healer in the New Testament.**

                                         Exodus 15:26

                                         Matthew 9:35

                                         Luke 4:18

(5) **Physical healing, health, and well-being was obtained for you by Jesus on the cross.**

                                         1 Peter 2:24

                                       Galatians 3:13, 14

God made Jesus carry to the cross all your pains, ailments, sicknesses, physical infirmities, and afflictions.

- Freedom from sin's curse was covered at Calvary and at the same time, by the same sacrifice, on the same cross, freedom from every pain, sickness, and all diseases that man has ever suffered or will suffer was obtained by Christ's shed blood!

If God laid all your pains and sicknesses on Jesus, then why should He expect you to carry any sickness or pain in your body today?

1 John 3:8 tells us that Jesus came to redeem and deliver your spirit, your mind, and your physical body from ALL the destructive works of the devil.

(6) **Sickness does not glorify the Lord;** it's being healed and staying well that glorifies God.                           1 Corinthians 6:19, 20

**The devil and his demons are the authors of all sickness,** disease, pain and human suffering. Let the Word of God settle that fact. Accept the Bible as your only textbook!

3 John 2 in the Wuest Translation says, **"Be continually having good health."**

This is the will of God for your life.

If you are continually living in good health, then that means your body is well, strong,

# Christ The Healer

**PERSONAL NOTES**

free from sickness — no pains, no illnesses, no chronic ailments. You will have DIVINE HEALTH.

The truth of the Bible will heal, deliver, and free you!

The Bible is the answer for every problem in the three-fold existence of man: Spirit, Soul, Body.

Jesus came and paid the price to redeem us in all three parts of the make-up of man.

Jesus redeemed us spiritually, soulishly, and physically.

Jesus redeemed us from all sickness and brought us into all the blessings of Abraham.

Jesus returned man back to his original condition before the fall and before sin entered.

*"He sent His word and healed them, And delivered them from their destructions."*

**Psalm 107:20**

The truth of God's Word heals us, delivers us, and sets us free from all sickness, making our bodies well.

Don't forget Psalm 103:3 — the benefit of healing.

Don't allow Satan's lies to hold you in bondage. He will attempt to convince you that God has something to do with sickness, pain, or physical affliction.

*"But He, knowing their thoughts, said to them: 'Every kingdom divided against itself is brought to desolation, and a house divided against a house falls."*

**Luke 11:17**

If God sends sickness or puts sickness on people, and Jesus died to heal us of all sickness, and He came as the Healer of suffering humanity, wouldn't that be confusion? Wouldn't that be a house divided against itself?

*"I will above everything else that you continually be prospering financially and that you continually live in good health to the degree that your soul is prospering."*

**3 John 2 (Greek New Testament)**

God's will for you is crystal clear.

**God's will is:**

(1)  Continual financial prosperity.

(2)  Continual good health.

(3)  Continual prosperity in your soul.

# LESSON: 8                              How To Minister Healing

**PERSONAL NOTES**

**KEY VERSE:**     Acts 3:6          *"Then Peter said, 'Silver and gold I do not have, but what I do have I give you: In the name of Jesus Christ of Nazareth, rise up and walk.'"*

**KEY TRUTH:**     It is God's will for you to flow in His healing power and be a miracle-working instrument in the hands of God. Every believer in the body of Christ is to be the hands of Jesus extended to the sick, suffering, and afflicted of our generation.

## THE SCRIPTURAL BASIS FOR THE HEALING MINISTRY

We need to clearly understand the Bible message of Healing:

* that it is God's Will for all to be healed.

* that the devil is behind sickness and human suffering.

* that Jesus is still the Healer today.

* that Jesus is the same today as He was in Matthew, Mark, Luke, and John.

* that in JESUS' NAME, by the power of the Holy Spirit we can heal the sick.

* that it is the Will of God to heal everybody.

The best time to learn, study, and know about divine healing is when you are well and healthy, not when you are fighting a cancer.

### Number 1
**Divine healing in the ministry of Jesus.**          Matthew 4:23, 24

Matthew 9:35

Matthew 14:14

God, revealed in the person of Jesus, came as the Healer of sick, suffering humanity.

Seventy percent of the ministry of Jesus involved healing the sick, casting out demons, and manifesting the miraculous.

### Number 2
**Jesus trained, equipped, and commissioned His twelve disciples to go out and heal the sick.**

Matthew 10:1, 7, 8

Mark 3:14, 15

Mark 6:7, 13

Luke 9:1, 2, 6

# How To Minister Healing

**PERSONAL NOTES**

### Number 3

Jesus commissioned and empowered the seventy disciples to minister divine healing to the sick.

Luke 10:1, 9, 17-20

### Number 4

Jesus has commissioned every believer — the whole church — with the ministry of healing.

Matthew 28:18-20

Mark 16:17, 18

John 14:12

After His Resurrection, Jesus transferred His miracle healing power to the whole church and gave all believers authority over all sickness and demon spirits.

Divine healing is included in the Great Commission and is to be preached as part of the Gospel.

## HEALING IN THE NEW TESTAMENT CHURCH

(1) Healing of the 40 year old beggar crippled from birth.        Acts 3:1-8, 16

(2) Healing of the multitudes in the streets of Jerusalem.        Acts 5:15, 16

(3) Healing, miracles, and deliverances took place at
    the revival in Samaria.        Acts 8:5-7

(4) Aeneas miraculously healed after being paralyzed
    for eight years.        Acts 9:32-35

(5) God's healing power healed a crippled man at Lystra.        Acts 14:7-10

(6) Divine healing through anointed prayer cloths.        Acts 19:11, 12

(7) Eutychus raised from the dead.        Acts 20:9-12

(8) Healing of many sick people on the island of Malta.        Acts 28:3-9

## STEPS TO RECEIVING HEALING

**What to do before prayer for healing:**

(a) Make sure there is no sin in your life.

> *"If we confess our sins, He is faithful and just to forgive us our sins and to cleanse us from all unrighteousness."*
>
> 1 John 1:9

(b) Forgive others, so you can be forgiven.

> *"And whenever you stand praying, if you have anything against anyone, forgive him, that your Father in Heaven may also forgive you your trespasses."*
>
> Mark 11:25

# How To Minister Healing

(c) Have scriptures to back up your faith.

*"Now this is the confidence that we have in Him, that if we ask anything according to His will, He hears us.*
*And if we know that He hears us, whatever we ask, we know that we have the petitions that we have asked of Him."*

1 John 5:14, 15

(d) Be prepared to believe you will receive.

*"Therefore I say to you, whatever things you ask when you pray, believe that you receive them, and you will have them."*

Mark 11:24

(e) Be prepared to immediately act in faith.

*"For as the body without the spirit is dead, so faith without works is dead also."*

James 2:26

**What to do during prayer for healing:**

(a) See yourself healed.

*"...while we do not look at the things which are seen, but at the things which are not seen. For the things which are seen are temporary, but the things which are not seen are eternal."*

2 Corinthians 4:18

(b) Release your faith.

*"Jesus said to him, 'Go your way; your son lives.' So the man believed the word that Jesus spoke to him... So the father knew that it was at the same hour in which Jesus said to him, 'Your son Lives.' And he himself believed, and his whole household."*

John 4:50, 53

(c) Begin to thank God for it.

*"...with thanksgiving, let your requests be made..."*

Philippians 4:6

**What to do after prayer for healing:**

(a) Meditate daily on the healing Scriptures and protect your thought life.

Philippians 4:8

(b) Boldly confess your healing and hold fast to your confession of faith.

Revelation 2:25

(c) Be steadfast and resist the devil, in Jesus name, against all lying symptoms that try and come back on your body.

Revelation 12:11

# How To Minister Healing

**PERSONAL NOTES**

(d) Feed your faith by regularly attending church services and listening to teaching tapes on healing and faith.

**Romans 10:17**

**GOD'S PROVISION FOR HEALING:**

**Number 1** is the Word of God.

**Number 2** is the Cross of Christ.

**Number 3** is the Name of Jesus.

In learning how to heal the sick, you will have to practice persistence in ministering to the sick because not every single person you pray for will be healed or get healed instantly.

Persistence and continually ministering to the sick will increase your experience and your faith in the healing ministry.

Don't look at your lack of results. Look to Jesus. Keep your eyes on Him!

There is no such thing as an INSTANT, "QUICK" OVERNIGHT SUCCESS in the Bible.

## VITAL KEYS IN THE HEALING MINISTRY

**The Key of Biblical Knowledge**

We must know what the Bible teaches about sickness and healing.

**The Key of God's Anointing**

The power that heals is Holy Spirit power.

**The Key of Spiritual Preparation**

You must spend time in communion with God. Private prayer comes before public ministry.

**The Key of Obedience**

You make up your mind to obey the New Testament Scriptures and the Great Commission of Mark, Chapter 16.

**The Key of Compassion**

This was the key to the ministry of Jesus.

**The Key of Faith in Jesus' Name**

Exercise the Power of Attorney. Use the name of Jesus which is the name above all disease. Use the name above ALL NAMES!

**The Key of Persistence**

You must stay true to your task, committed to regularly praying for the sick. Look for opportunities to minister to sick people.

# How To Minister Healing

## METHODS OF MINISTERING HEALING

God wants sick people healed and He has provided at least ten different avenues whereby they can receive healing.

### Number 1

Anointing the sick with oil, in obedience to James 5:14, 15.

*"And they cast out many demons, and anointed with oil many who were sick, and healed them."*

Mark 6:13

### Number 2

Healing the sick through the gifts of the Spirit.      1 Corinthians 12:7-11

John 5:1-9

Gifts of healings and words of knowledge working together are powerful.

*"God also bearing witness both with signs and wonders, with various miracles, and gifts of the Holy Spirit, according to His own will?"*

Hebrews 2:4

### Number 3

Praying the prayer of agreement.      Matthew 18:18, 19

### Number 4

The laying on of hands, in obedience to the Great Commission.

Mark 16:18

Luke 4:40

*"They will take up serpents; and if they drink anything deadly, it will by no means hurt them; they will lay hands on the sick, and they will recover."*

Mark 16:18

Laying on of hands as a point of contact releases the LAW OF CONTACT AND TRANSMISSION to work, which sends God's Power into the disease to destroy it and undo the works of the devil.

### Number 5

Healing by the spoken word—the command of faith.      John 4:46-53

Matthew 8:8, 9

Mark 11:23

Psalm 107:20

# How To Minister Healing

**PERSONAL NOTES**

*"The centurion answered and said, 'Lord, I am not worthy that You should come under my roof. But only speak a word, and my servant will be healed.*

*For I also am a man under authority, having soldiers under me. And I say to this one, 'Go, and he goes; and to another, 'Come,' and he comes; and to my servant, 'Do this,' and he does it.'"*

Matthew 8:8, 9

*"For assuredly, I say to you, whoever says to this mountain, 'Be removed and be cast into the sea,' and does not doubt in his heart, but believes that those things he says will be done, he will have whatever he says."*

Mark 11:23

*"He sent His word and healed them, And delivered them from their destructions."*

Psalm 107:20

Jesus said with our words we can curse sickness and command it to wither up.

Jesus said we have authority to speak to the mountain of sickness and command it to go – speak to it.

## Number 6

Asking the Father in Jesus' Name.

John 16:23, 24

Philippians 2:9, 10

We have the power to heal and drive out disease in the MIGHTY NAME OF JESUS.

## Number 7

Partaking of the Lord's supper, receiving Holy Communion.

1 Peter 2:24

1 Corinthians 10:16

Psalm 103:2, 3

1 Corinthians 11:23-31

*"Who Himself bore our sins in His own body on the tree, that we, having died to sins, might live for righteousness – by whose stripes you were healed."*

1 Peter 2:24

*"The cup of blessing which we bless, is it not the communion of the blood of Christ? The bread which we break, is it not the communion of the body of Christ."*

1 Corinthians 10:16

# How To Minister Healing

*"Bless the Lord, O my soul, And forget not all His benefits: Who forgives all your iniquities, Who heals all your diseases."*

Psalm 103:2, 3

We must remember our benefits because of CHRIST'S FINISHED WORK.

## Number 8

The use of anointed prayer cloths.                     Acts 19:11, 12

Praying over handkerchiefs or cloths "CHARGES" them with the healing power of God, so as they are carried to the sick, the ANOINTING will go into them to HEAL and UNDO SATAN'S WORKS.

## Number 9

Taking God's Word as medicine.

The individual believer who is sick can take the healing Scriptures himself and daily read them, meditate upon them, and speak them out loud.

This allows the healing virtue in God's Word to work like divine medicine in your body.

Proverbs 4:13, 20-22

Psalm 107:20

## Number 10

Casting out the Spirit of Infirmity.                     Matthew 8:16

Mark 16:17

Acts 10:38

*"When evening had come, they brought to Him many who were demon-possessed. And He cast out the spirits with a word, and healed all who were sick."*

Matthew 8:16

*"And these signs will follow those who believe: In My name they will cast out demons; they will speak with new tongues."*

Mark 16:17

*"How God anointed Jesus of Nazareth with the Holy Spirit and with power, who went about doing good and healing all who were oppressed by the devil, for God was with Him."*

Acts 10:38

Many sicknesses are caused by demon spirits, such as blindness, deafness, arthritis, crooked spine (scoliosis), cancer, leukemia, etc.

IN JESUS' NAME we can bind and cast out the spirit of disease and infirmity.

# How To Minister Healing

**PERSONAL NOTES**

All demons are subject to believers IN THE NAME OF JESUS.

**Matthew 12:22, 28**
**Luke 13:11-13, 16**

In this end time revival every believer in Christ is commissioned and anointed with the power of God to minister healing, deliverance, and salvation.

## FIVE PURPOSES OF THE HEALING MINISTRY

(1) To show God's love, compassion, and mercy, and relieve human suffering.

(2) To demonstrate that God's kingdom has arrived.

(3) To give evidence that the Gospel is true and that Jesus is alive.

(4) To draw people to Jesus and bring them to salvation.

(5) To bring glory and honor to God.

## HOW YOU CAN MINISTER TO THE SICK

*"Most assuredly, I say to you, he who believes in Me, the works that I do he will do also; and greater works than these he will do, because I go to My Father."*
**John 14:12**

You must believe that Jesus has called and anointed you to bring God's healing power to the sick, and be committed to regularly praying for the sick in obedience to Mark, Chapter 16.

### Number 1
**Prepare yourself for ministry to the sick by spending time in prayer and reading the healing Scriptures.**

**Acts 4:13, 29-31**

- All ministry and moving in the Holy Spirit is only effective and dynamic if it flows out of your daily relationship with the Holy Spirit.

- Public ministry flows out of, and depends upon, your private ministry unto the Lord.

### Number 2
**Always seek to minister to people with God's love and compassion.**

**Matthew 14:14**
**Galatians 5:6**
**1 Corinthians 13:1-3**

# How To Minister Healing

## Number 3

Locate the person by asking questions before you pray for them. For example:

- How long have you been sick?
- Where is the pain?
- What does your doctor say about the illness?
- Do you believe it is God's will to heal you?
- Do you believe Jesus heals today?
- Are you scheduled for an operation?
- Do you have any unforgiveness in your heart towards anyone?

While asking these questions, listen for the Holy Spirit to give you additional information.

## Number 4

Follow the example of Jesus and share God's Word with the person who is sick before praying for them.

Matthew 4:23

Matthew 9:35

Romans 10:17

Never lay hands on the sick or pray for them, without first of all teaching God's Word about healing.

WHY DO WE SHARE GOD'S WORD FIRST?

(1) Because the Word of God creates faith in peoples' hearts.

(2) The Word of God cures unbelief.

(3) The Word of God destroys all doubts in peoples' minds.

(4) The Word of God renews minds with accurate thinking. God's Word eliminates questions, wrong doctrines, and faulty theology.

(5) The Word of God releases the life-giving power of the Holy Spirit.

## Number 5

Pray for the person in the Name of Jesus, claiming specific scriptures:

- Anointing with oil                        James 5:14-15
- Laying on of hands                      Mark 16:18
- Praying the prayer of agreement     Matthew 18:19

## Number 6

After prayer, give them after-care, encourage them to continue in God's Word.

Proverbs 4:20-22

# How To Minister Healing

**PERSONAL NOTES**

- Give them healing verses to read every day.
- Give them tapes on healing.
- Arrange for them to attend church services.
- Tell them how to resist the devil. (James 4:7)

**REMEMBER:**

Divine healing and the ministry of healing is acting in obedience to what the New Testament says – the Great Commission. You are obeying Jesus, the Head of the Church, when you minister to the sick.

God's Word promises that signs and wonders are definitely going to follow you because you share the anointed Word of God without any compromise. (Mark 16:17-20)

LAYING ON OF HANDS IS A KEY METHOD IN HEALING THE SICK.

Start practicing your authority in Jesus' Name – ears, backs, eyes, muscles, disease, all sickness and pains respond to and obey the Name of Jesus.

Healing is released in the Name of Jesus through the believer's hands by the power of the Holy Spirit.

SIGNS AND WONDERS OCCUR IN THE NAME OF JESUS.

HEALING AND MIRACLES MANIFEST IN THE NAME OF JESUS.

Signs and Wonders follow New Testament believers – the "believing ones."

Your belief is vital to moving in signs and wonders, and healing the sick.

## MINISTERING LIKE JESUS

In studying the ministry of Jesus and reading the Gospels, we see that:

- Jesus laid hands upon the sick. He touched the sick and the anointing in Him was released to the sick.                                   (Luke 4:40, 41)
- Jesus spoke the Word of authority. He commanded sickness, fever, and spirits of infirmity to go – and they obeyed.                   (Luke 13:11-13)

In Jesus' Name, lay your hands upon the part of the person's body that is sick (deaf ears, heart problems, kidney infection, back pain). As you lay on hands, release the resurrection power of God to heal, restore, and make whole.

In Jesus' Name, speak the Word of authority and command the disease, the illness, the pain, and the demons of infirmity to leave.

Lay hands on the afflicted area (ear, nose, eyes, feet, heart) and direct the healing energy of God to the area which is sick.                   (Matthew 20:34)

The Bible doesn't say to lay hands on the heads of the sick and heal them.

# How To Minister Healing

Rather, we need to lay hands in Jesus' Name on the **specific area** which is hurting, diseased, or afflicted (e. g. nose, ears, chest, right leg, lower back, eyes, etc.).

By doing this in Jesus' Name, you are releasing the flow of God's healing power and resurrection life right into the part of the body that needs healing.

The power of God can go directly into the sick part of the person's body. For example, if someone's right ankle has been injured, lay hands on that area and send God's healing power into it. Very often people will go down under the power of God as you pray.

As a blood bought member of the body of Christ, your hands are an extension of the hands of Jesus.

- Healing the sick and ministering with results will involve your persistence, patience, and continual practice of ministry to the sick.
- PERSISTENCE is a great key to moving in God's power. Don't get discouraged and stop because you do not see all the sick people you minister to get healed.

Jesus laid hands on the sick and He commanded the disease to cease, and the affliction and demons to come out. He commanded them to be healed.

Jesus spoke the word of command with authority.

## Key Number 1
**LAYING ON OF HANDS**
This releases the energy of God to drive out devils and disease!

## Key Number 2
**THE SPOKEN COMMAND OF AUTHORITY**
- Command sick bodies to be healed.
- Command demons of affliction to leave.
- Command pain to stop.
- Lay hands on people, with authority.
- Command the sick to be well, with authority.
- Command demons to leave, with authority.

Don't act like a wimp or be wishy-washy about it! Be bold!

Some healings are instantaneous (that is, a miracle).

Some healings are gradual, progressive – a process (two hours, two days, two weeks).

We are CONTAINERS, CARRIERS, AND CONDUCTORS of the healing power of God.

Every time you lay hands on the sick, you are giving God the opportunity to display His power and show His strength.

Speak to disease, demons, pain, and affliction. They obey the command of faith.

Laying on of hands releases the power of God into the sick person's body. When God's

# How To Minister Healing

**PERSONAL NOTES**

power and anointing goes in, then sickness and disease go out.

The person being healed – receiving healing – MUST put their faith into action.

Get them to do something:

- THROAT PROBLEMS/BLOCKAGE:  Drink water
- HAND CRIPPLED WITH ARTHRITIS:  Move hand
- BACK INJURY:  Bend over

"Move your shoulder, your arm, your neck", etc.

**Psalm 42:11 (Living Bible) says, *"EXPECT GOD TO ACT."***

With the command of faith "IN THE NAME OF JESUS," you can command:

- Muscles and nerves to relax.
- Back injuries to be reversed and all vertebrae to be healed.
- Tension to leave.
- Arthritis to come out and leave every joint in the body.
- Legs and limbs to grow out in perfect length.
- Bones and discs to move into place.
- Migraine headaches to stop and not return.
- Neck and shoulders to adjust perfectly.
- Pain and affliction to go.
- Deaf ears to be opened.
- Cancerous tumors and growths to die and disappear.

If you will just step out in faith and practice your authority IN JESUS' NAME, God will heal people from all kinds of sickness, including doing creative miracles.

## DEALING WITH DEMONS

Scripturally, we do not have to be, nor should we be afraid of demon spirits, because they are actually afraid of New Testament believers.

Why?

Because we have been given all power and all authority over the devil and demon spirits.

*"You are of God, little children, and have overcome them, because He who is in you is greater than he who is in the world."*

**1 John 4:4**

*"Behold, I give you the authority to trample on serpents and scorpions, and over all the power of the enemy, and nothing shall by any means hurt you."*

**Luke 10:19**

# How To Minister Healing

*"For God has not given us a spirit of fear, but of power and of love and of a sound mind."*

2 Timothy 1:7

As the church of the Lord Jesus Christ, we are empowered and commissioned to do three things we should practice continually:

**(1) Preach and proclaim the kingdom Gospel**

**(2) Heal the sick**

**(3) Cast out demons and deliver the demonized**

Jesus Christ came for this purpose: to destroy the works of the devil.                                            1 John 3:8

We have the authority in Jesus' name to expose and expel demon spirits.                                         James 4:7

We need to know Biblically how to deal with the devil and demons.

We are to free people from the bondage of the devil.

The NAME OF JESUS is above every name.

The NAME OF JESUS is above all other names.

The NAME OF JESUS is above all disease.

The NAME OF JESUS is above all sickness.

The NAME OF JESUS is above all affliction.

The NAME OF JESUS is above all pain and infirmity.

The NAME OF JESUS is above all demon spirits.

Demons attack the individual in two major ways:

(1) **THE BODY** with disease, physical affliction, and pain.

(2) **THE MIND** with fear, oppression, depression, lust, suicide, and strongholds of obsessive and compulsive desires.

All sickness, all disease, all pain, all fear, and all demon spirits are subject to the name of Jesus and must obey the name of Jesus.

Believe you have authority over the devil in Jesus' Name.

Act on the authority you have over demon spirits IN JESUS' NAME by CASTING them out and setting people free.

Practice your authority in Jesus' Name by ministering to the sick and freeing the demonized.

IMPORTANT

• The more sick people you pray for, the more healings will manifest.

• The more you cast out demons, the more success you will have.

# How To Minister Healing

© 1994 The Believer's School of Training, Rev. Norman K. Robertson

**PERSONAL NOTES**

- The more you do it, the more anointing you will have.

You have power and authority over all demons. Believe and act on that fact. You can depend on the Word of God, the anointing of the Holy Spirit and the name of Jesus to get results!

You do not have to be afraid of any demons.

Believe and expect demons to come out of people as you use the name of Jesus.

Whatever you tell demons to do, as an anointed minister with the authority of Jesus, and in His name, demons will obey your words. Demons will do what you tell them.

You can bind them by the power of the Holy Spirit in Jesus' name.

You can break their power over peoples' lives.

You can make them shut up. Tell them to shut up.

You can cast out spirits of disease, fear, infirmity.

You can command them to come out of people in Jesus' name.

WHEN DEALING WITH DEMONS, DO NOT DOUBT GOD'S WORD OR THE AUTHORITY YOU HAVE IN THE NAME OF JESUS.

Yes! Demons have power, but they DO NOT have power over us.

Cancer, terminal illnesses, AIDS, and incurable diseases are caused by demon spirits of infirmity.

All sickness is in the earth and afflicting the human race today because Satan brought it here.

All incurable diseases involve demon spirits lodged in the body or oppressing the body.

Jesus did not ask demons for their names or have a conversation with them. Jesus told them two things in Mark 1:25:

(1) SHUT UP
(2) COME OUT

We need the Holy Spirit to show us through the gift of discerning of spirits what kind of demon spirits are oppressing and afflicting people. We must be guided by the Holy Spirit and be obedient to His instructions.

Jesus identified, recognized, and cast out demon spirits for what they did to people:

| | |
|---|---|
| BLINDNESS | Blind spirits |
| DEAFNESS | Deaf spirits |
| CROOKED SPINE (SCOLIOSIS) | Spirit of infirmity |
| DUMBNESS | Dumb spirits |
| ARTHRITIS | Spirit of infirmity |
| EPILEPSY/LUNATIC/INSANE | Spirit of insanity |

# How To Minister Healing

Usually the type of disease or affliction a person has is the same as the demon spirit causing the disease. Be sensitive to the leading of the Holy Spirit.

| | |
|---|---|
| DRUG ABUSE | Spirit of addiction |
| ARTHRITIS | Spirit of arthritis & infirmity |
| DEAFNESS | Spirit of deafness |
| CANCER | Spirit of cancer & spirit of death |
| HOMOSEXUALITY | Spirit of perversion & homosexuality |

Call out by name, identify the demons by how they are afflicting people, or by what they are doing to people and CAST THEM OUT.

The key is to minister in the power of the Holy Spirit, knowing your authority in Jesus' name, without any fear of them. They are afraid of you.

You don't need to spend three, five, or ten hours trying to cast demons out of people. Demons obeyed Jesus immediately!

**Exercise your New Testament authority today and remember it is the anointing that sets the captives free.**

# Response To Truth
*Lessons 7 and 8*

**IMPORTANT:** *Set aside 15 minutes each day to read and review these study notes until your mind is renewed to the reality that Christ IS the healer and He wants to use you in the ministry of healing.*

© 1994 The Believer's School of Training, Rev. Norman K. Robertson

**PERSONAL NOTES**

## KEY QUESTIONS

(1) Name five Biblical methods for ministering to the sick.

(2) Are demon spirits responsible for sickness and disease?  Please explain.

(3) Give three reasons why Christ heals today.

(4) What is the difference between mercy and compassion?

(5) What are the steps in receiving healing?

(6) How do you know it is always God's will to heal the sick and afflicted?

## MEMORY WORK

Proverbs 4:20-22

Matthew 9:35

James 5:14, 15

## PERSONAL APPLICATION

(1) How have these dynamic healing truths affected your life?

(2) Have you recently ministered to someone who was sick and God healed them?  What happened?

(3) Have you prayed and asked the Lord to use you in the healing ministry?

(4) Take action against the works of the devil; be committed to praying for sick people on a regular basis.

## RECOMMENDED READING:

F. F. Bosworth, *Christ The Healer*

Kenneth E. Hagin, *Healing Belongs To Us*

Gordon Lindsay, *Bible Days Are Here Again*

Rodney M. Howard-Browne, *Flowing in the Holy Ghost*

# LESSON: 9                                      Authority Over Demon Spirits

**KEY VERSE:**    Luke 8:2    *"And certain women who had been healed of evil spirits and infirmities – Mary called Magdalene, out of whom had come seven demons."*

**KEY TRUTH:**    Christians need to clearly understand what the Bible teaches about demon spirits and how to deal with them.

## WHAT ARE DEMONS AND WHERE DO THEY COME FROM?

### (1) THE PRE-ADAMIC RACE

Most Bible scholars agree that between Genesis 1:1 and Genesis 1:2 there is a TIME GAP of an undetermined period in the history of the universe, before the creation of Adam. It could possibly be millions or billions of years. This explains the scientific evidence about fossils, dinosaurs, the ice age, etc.

Scriptures such as Isaiah 45:18; Jeremiah 4:23-26; Isaiah 24:1; 2 Peter 3:5-7, indicate that the earth before Adam was populated with nations, kingdoms, cities, and inhabitants. Lucifer was God's ruler over the PRE-ADAMIC earth, and through pride he led a rebellion against Heaven and the Lord God of the universe. Along with Lucifer, in his rebellion, was one-third of the Angels and the inhabitants of the PRE-ADAMIC earth.

> **Ezekiel 28:12-19**
>
> **Isaiah 14:12-17**
>
> **Luke 10:18**
>
> **Revelation 12:9**

God's judgment upon the rebels is the reason for SATAN, FALLEN ANGELS, and DEMON SPIRITS as well as the devastation of the original earth by a flood and its lying in a chaotic mess for millions of years.

**Genesis 1:1** is a description of the original perfect earth.

**Genesis 1:2** is a picture of the earth that became a ruined, formless wasteland, plunged into darkness because of God's judgement upon Lucifer's rebellion.

**Genesis 1:3-31** is an account of God's re-creation or restoration of planet earth.

### (2) GOD DID NOT CREATE SATAN OR EVIL

God is a good God. He is always good all of the time. He is not responsible for evil, sin, sickness, or any type of suffering that plagues mankind. God is the Creator of the universe. (John 1:1-3; Colossians 1:16, 17). He is the One who created Lucifer as a beautiful, pure, and glorious Archangel. Lucifer was sinless, holy, and perfect. He led the worship in Heaven and ruled over the PRE-ADAMIC earth. By his own decision, Lucifer yielded to envy and pride and led a rebellion against the God of Heaven. Through his own corruption and iniquity, Lucifer became a fallen angelic being – SATAN – whose name means "THE ENEMY."

# Authority Over Demon Spirits

**PERSONAL NOTES**

## (3) DEMONS ARE NOT FALLEN ANGELS

I.  Demons are not human spirits of the departed dead.

II. Demons are not the fallen angels who fell with Satan in his rebellion against Heaven.

There are distinct differences between fallen angels and demon spirits.

    (a) Angels have wings and demons do not.

                                                     **Daniel 9:21**

    (b) Fallen angels inhabit the heavenlies, not the earth.

                                                     **Ephesians 2:2**

                                                  **Ephesians 6:12**

    (c) Demon spirits are on the earth and are never seen in the heavenlies.

                                                   **Matthew 12:43**

                                                   **Mark 5:1-13**

    (d) Angels have bodies of their own and demons do not have bodies.

                                                   **Genesis 19:1-5**

                                                **Matthew 12:43-45**

    (e) The Scriptures reveal that angels never seek to enter or inhabit another body, while demons have an intense craving to enter and occupy a body, whether human or animal.

                                                   **Mark 5:11-13**

III. Demons are the disembodied spirit beings of the PRE-ADAMIC race.

    The Bible calls them EVIL SPIRITS, UNCLEAN SPIRITS, AND DEMONS.

    They are real personalities, able to think, speak, and act, carrying out Satan's evil plans and purposes against mankind.

## WHAT ARE THE CHARACTERISTICS OF DEMON SPIRITS?

**DESCRIPTION OF DEMONS:**

A. Demons are real personalities. They are intelligent and wise, having a will and able to act according to their evil natures.

                                                   **Matthew 8:29-31**

                                                   **Luke 4:33-35**

                                                   **James 2:19**

                                               **Matthew 12:43-45**

B. Demons are spirit beings – invisible persons without bodies, always seeking to enter and manifest their evil desires through human beings.

                                                   **Matthew 8:16**

                                                   **Luke 9:38-42**

# Authority Over Demon Spirits

**C.** Demons possess supernatural strength and they are large in number.

Mark 5:1-13

**D.** Demons can speak and they have feelings, emotions, and desires – all the characteristics of personality.

Luke 4:41

Acts 8:7

Matthew 8:28-31

**E.** Demons have names. The Bible speaks of deaf spirits, dumb spirits, blind spirits, spirits of infirmity, fortune-telling spirits.

Mark 9:25

Matthew 12:22

Luke 13:11

Acts 16:16

**F.** Demons have knowledge. They know who Jesus is. They know of their future judgment and damnation. They know which believers have power over them.

Luke 4:34, 41

Matthew 8:29

Acts 19:13-16

Luke 10:17

**G.** Demons are not human for they can possess men and be cast out.

Mark 16:17

Matthew 12:43-45

**H.** Demons are symbolized in Scripture in terms which express their evil nature:

(1) As Fowls of the Air — Matthew 13:4, 19

(2) As Serpents and Vipers — Matthew 23:33

(3) As Unclean Frogs — Revelation 16:13, 14

(4) As Unclean Birds in a cage — Revelation 18:1-3

(5) As Locusts from the bottomless pit — Revelation 9:1-10

**I.** Demons at this present time dwell on the earth. They are not in Hell and will not go there until the future judgment.

Matthew 12:43-45

Matthew 8:29

**J.** Demons vary in strength and power.

Matthew 12:43-45

Mark 9:28, 29

# Authority Over Demon Spirits

**PERSONAL NOTES**

**K.** Demons have willpower and they resist and fight against surrender.

> **Matthew 8:28, 29**
>
> **Matthew 12:44**
>
> **Luke 8:27-32**

**L.** Demons are subject to the sovereignty of the Lord Jesus Christ. They are subject to the authority of Jesus' name and they must submit to the power of the Holy Spirit.

> **Matthew 8:16**
>
> **Luke 4:40, 41**
>
> **Matthew 12:28**
>
> **1 John 4:4**
>
> **Mark 16:17**
>
> **1 Peter 3:22**

## THE OPERATION AND ACTIVITIES OF DEMON SPIRITS

What does the Bible reveal about the work of demons and what they can do to people?

### (1) Demons are the source of sickness and disease.

The Bible calls sickness bondage of Satan. Luke 13:16.

The Bible calls sickness the oppression of the devil. Acts 10:38.

*"When evening had come, they brought to Him many who were demon-possessed. And He cast out the spirits with a word, and healed all who were sick."*

> **Matthew 8:16**

*And that very hour He cured many people of their infirmities, afflictions, and evil spirits; and to many who were blind He gave sight."*

> **Luke 7:21**

The Bible reveals that demons are responsible for:

| | |
|---|---|
| Blindness | Matthew 12:22 |
| Deafness | Mark 9:25 |
| Dumbness | Matthew 9:32, 33 |
| Crippling Arthritis and Deformity | Luke 13:11 |
| Fever | Luke 4:39 |
| Epilepsy | Matthew 17:14-18 |
| All types of sickness and disease | Matthew 4:23, 24 |

# Authority Over Demon Spirits

(2)  **Demons are the source of temptation and enticement to sin.**

> James 1:13-15
>
> John 8:34

Demons carry out the will and instructions of Satan, which is to make sin look attractive, inviting, exciting, and irresistible, to bring man into bondage.

(3)  **Demons attack and wage war against the minds of men with fear, oppression, and depression. They are responsible for emotional and mental breakdown, insanity, and suicide.**

> 2 Timothy 1:7
>
> Isaiah 61:3
>
> Mark 5:1-5, 15

(4)  **Demons deceive. They promote false doctrines, false religions, and false prophets and seek to blind men from the truth of the Gospel.**

> 1 Timothy 4:1, 2
>
> 2 Corinthians 4:4
>
> 2 Corinthians 11: 3, 4

Jesus warned us that the last days would be characterized by a great increase in religious deception.

(5)  **Demons (called in scripture unclean spirits) ensnare and enslave people with unclean habits such as alcoholism, drug abuse, smoking, sexual immorality, perversion, and pornography, etc.**

> John 8:34
>
> Romans 6:16

(6)  **Demons defile people by drawing them into bondage of the occult, witchcraft, astrology, and Satanism.**

> Deuteronomy 18:9-12
>
> Leviticus 19:31
>
> Isaiah 47:12-14

Demon spirits are evil, malignant, cruel, and wicked spirits and are out to destroy you.

**TWO COMMON ERRORS CHRISTIANS AND MINISTERS MAKE ABOUT DEMONS:**

<u>Number 1.</u> Seeing demons everywhere and behind everything (e.g. coffee demons, chewing gum demons, etc.).

# Authority Over Demon Spirits

**PERSONAL NOTES**

<u>Number 2.</u> Thinking that there are no demons or ignoring them altogether.

*"Be sober, be vigilant; because your adversary the devil walks about like a roaring lion, seeking whom he may devour. Resist him, steadfast in the faith..."*
1 Peter 5:8, 9

All Christians are the target of demon spirits and Satanic attacks.

The child of God cannot be demon possessed, however, Christians can have demons.

Realize the following facts:

(a) **Your spirit** is born again and indwelt by the Holy Spirit.

(b) **Your mind** is not born again and has to be renewed by the Word of God. Your thought life must be protected. Otherwise, demons will invade and oppress your mind.

(c) **Your body** is not born again but has to be presented daily as a living sacrifice to God. Otherwise, through the lusts of the flesh, demons will come in.

## DEMONS VERSUS THE FLESH

There is a difference between the works of the flesh and demonic activity.

There is a lot of confusion, neglect, and misinformation in the realm of demonic teaching and spiritual warfare.

The real truth is that a Christian cannot be demon possessed, but a Christian can have a demon.

A Christian can have demonic activity in his life: depression, obsession, oppression, but NEVER possession! The devil is NOT greater than the indwelling Holy Spirit.

**Ephesians 1:13**
**1 John 4:4**

The word "possession" means a complete take-over – spirit, soul, and body. It means ownership and control!

Demonic activity in the life of a believer is due to giving the enemy a place in your life. You open the door!

*"'Be angry, and do not sin', do not let the sun go down on your wrath, nor give place to the devil."*
**Ephesians 4:26, 27**

*"Therefore submit to God. Resist the devil and he will flee from you."*
**James 4:7**

**KEY TRUTH:** The works of the flesh (maybe secret sins) yielded to, abided by, and embraced by Christians are decisions of the will, and give opportunity for the enemy to come in and build a stronghold.

# Authority Over Demon Spirits

For example:

- When we yield to and harbor bitterness in our lives.
- When we allow ourselves to compromise with the world.
- When we permit certain things into our lives.
- When we entertain fleshly thoughts.
- When we play around with sin.
- When we serve the works of the flesh.

At some point, known or unknown, demonic activity comes in through the works of the flesh and demons gain a stronghold in your life until they take you into captivity, and you are held in bondage by demons.

## THE WORKS OF THE FLESH EXPOSED AND IDENTIFIED

**KEY SCRIPTURES:** 1 Peter 2:11;  Romans 7:18;  Galatians 5:16, 19-21;
Matthew 15:19;  Mark 7:21;  Colossians 3:5-10;  Ephesians 4:17-24.

When the flesh is in control of our lives, it is characterized and manifested in different ways which the Bible calls THE WORKS OF THE FLESH.

## (1) ADULTERY

This refers to illicit sexual activity by an individual who is married to someone other than his sexual partner.

## (2) FORNICATION

This refers to unlawful sexual relations between single people. It also includes sexual perversion such as homosexuality.

## (3) UNCLEANNESS

This refers to impure sexual thoughts and desires.

## (4) LASCIVIOUSNESS/LICENTIOUSNESS

When unclean thoughts control the person, it is called "lasciviousness." This causes the person to seek after sexual activity, such as dirty magazines and movies. The lascivious person has given himself over to his sexual cravings.

## (5) IDOLATRY

In the day in which these verses were written, idolatry referred to the worship of graven images. Today it includes giving preeminence to anything other than God. It could be money, power, position, fame, glory, even a business, club, or amusement.

IDOLATRY is when a person elevates something to a higher position than God.

# Authority Over Demon Spirits

**PERSONAL NOTES**

## (6) WITCHCRAFT/SORCERY

In the Greek it is "pharmakeia," from which we derive our English word, "pharmacy." Witchcraft has always revolved around the use of drugs.

It is any involvement with the occult, spiritualism, and the practice of magic by yielding to evil spirits. The occult is the devil's supernatural.

## (7) HATRED

Hatred is defined as bitter dislike, malice, animosity, and ill will against someone. It is the tendency to hold grudges and resentment against someone.

Like lust, it is a mental sin.

Like all mental sins, hatred is a cancer. It harms the one it inhabits far more than the one to whom it is directed.

## (8) VARIANCE/CONTENTIONS

This refers to discord, dissension, quarreling, debating, and disputes. Variance describes people who always want to disagree.

## (9) EMULATIONS/JEALOUSIES

This is striving to excel at the expense of another person, seeking to surpass and outdo others. It is a competitive attitude, a spirit of rivalry that must be better than others.

It is trying to play "spiritual king of the mountain." It is an attitude that will not cooperate with others unless it gets its own way. We would call it ambition or rivalry.

## (10) WRATH

Wrath is the outward manifestation of inward hatred. It refers to emotional outbursts, explosions of anger.

## (11) STRIFE/SELFISH AMBITIONS

Strife simply means discord or disharmony.

Strife is a group-related activity. It manifests itself in temper tantrums, complaining, troublemaking. Its root source is lack of love.

## (12) SEDITIONS/DISSENSIONS

This is rebellion against governing authorities and stirring up strife in religion, government, the home, etc. It is causing divisions.

## (13) HERESIES

A heresy is any opinion which is contrary to God's Word.

It is false doctrine, any doctrine or teaching that is contrary to the Gospel of Christ.

# Authority Over Demon Spirits

## (14) ENVYING

Envying is an inward or mental sin. It is the attitude that "everyone gets a better break than me," or "I must have what that person has."

## (15) MURDERS

Notice that Paul does not say that it is "killing" which is wrong. Rather, murder is the sin. It is always condemned in the Word of God.

## (16) DRUNKENNESS

The Word of God has always condemned drunkenness, which is the excessive use of alcohol.

## (17) REVELING

This simply refers to wild parties, carousing, and brawling which usually accompany drunkenness.

## (18) AND SUCH LIKE

This is Paul's way of indicating that this list of sins on the part of a Christian is not inclusive. It is only a partial listing of the many manifestations of the flesh.

The works of the flesh are born in the will, and as you sin repeatedly, enjoy it, and give yourselves over to it repeatedly, e.g. sexual immorality, homosexuality, THEN demons enter and begin to drive you, oppress you, and dictate to you.

Demonic activity is compulsive behavior. In other words, you can no longer control yourself. You have lost all will power!

If you have any kind of compulsive behavior – anger, fear, jealousy, lust, sexual immorality – then you need deliverance because that thing has gone beyond the works of the flesh into demonic influence.

Compulsive behavior can be:

Compulsive jealousy

Compulsive anger and rage

Compulsive workaholic

Compulsive sexual things

Stubborn unforgiveness and hatred.

Compulsive means you are driven and consumed with that thing in your life.

You are HOOKED on pornography.

You are DRIVEN by lust.

You are HOOKED on cigarettes.

You have become DRUG DEPENDENT.

You are ADDICTED to food or to losing weight.

You are driven by ANGER and HATE.

# Authority Over Demon Spirits

**PERSONAL NOTES**

Any area of the flesh you are hooked on and cannot control is demonic activity present in your life.

Compulsive behavior = DEMONS and DEMONIC influence in your life.

Demonic activity is compulsive behavior. In other words, you can no longer control yourself. The thing in your life controls you.

So when character weaknesses such as anger, lying, greed, sexual things, jealousy, and envy, become strongholds in your life and compulsive behavior, then it has moved out from the realm of the flesh into demonic activity. Compulsive behavior is any uncontrolled desire.

In the Church today, there are **two extremes** taught which are error and false doctrine.

(1) Everything is the flesh and the believer's warfare is with the mind and the flesh. There is no problem with demonic activity.

(2) Everything is demons and deliverance and nothing to do with the flesh. Because of this extreme false teaching in many places the ministry of "deliverance," has fallen into disrepute.

We have to always stay "balanced," in the middle of the road, to avoid extreme teachings on any subject.

## THREE STEPS INTO DEMONIC INFLUENCE

*"It is actually reported that there is sexual immorality among you, and such sexual immorality as is not even named among the Gentiles — that a man has his father's wife! In the name of our Lord Jesus Christ, when you are gathered together, along with my spirit, with the power of our Lord Jesus Christ, deliver such a one to Satan for the destruction of the flesh, that his spirit may be saved in the day of the Lord Jesus."*

1 Corinthians 5:1, 4, 5

(1) When the works of the flesh begin to develop into an entrenched habit, it becomes a regular habit pattern.

(2) The habit then becomes compulsive behavior. It is out of control! Then you are trapped and can't straighten yourself out. You are being driven by compulsive behavior.

(3) The demons enter and establish strongholds in your life.

Deliverance ministry does not deal with the works of the flesh. It only frees you from demonic activity and compulsive behavior. It does not deal with your flesh problem.

That is why if you minister deliverance to someone, you have to instruct him on how to overcome the flesh and walk in the Spirit. Otherwise, the deliverance will not be maintained.

Remember, you cannot cast out the flesh! Romans Chapters 6, 7, and 8 tell us exactly what to do with our flesh.

# Authority Over Demon Spirits

## HOW CAN WE PROTECT OURSELVES FROM DEMON SPIRITS?

James 4:7          Psalm 91:1-16          Luke 10:17-19          1 Peter 5:8, 9

*"We know that whoever is born of God does not sin; but he who has been born of God keeps himself, and the wicked one does not touch him."*

1 John 5:18

We protect ourselves from demonic activity and influence by the following:

## Number 1

SHUT THE DOOR ON SATAN.
Give the devil no place in your life through sin or compromise with your flesh.

Ephesians 4:27

Stay off the devil's territory and don't make yourself vulnerable to temptation.

Stay away from places of sin – disco's, bars, night clubs, rock concerts, ungodly associations.

Don't open your mind to spirits of fear, unclean spirits, spirits of lust or violence. Be selective about books, T.V., videos, movies, etc.

Don't yield yourself to bad habits or bad attitudes.

Demon spirits are just waiting for you to give them the legal grounds to enter and control your life.

## Number 2

DAILY MAKE SURE YOU ARE WEARING THE WHOLE ARMOR OF GOD.
(All Seven Pieces, not just two or three).          Ephesians 6:10-18

## Number 3

WALK IN THE COVERING PROTECTION OF THE BLOOD OF JESUS.

Revelation 12:11

## Number 4

RESIST THE DEVIL BY SPEAKING THE WORD OF GOD AGAINST HIM IN JESUS' NAME.

James 4:7
Matthew 4:1-11

You must quote Scripture to the devil. Say, "IT IS WRITTEN..."

Don't allow the devil to harass you with wrong thoughts, lies, symptoms of sickness, or negative circumstances. Give Satan a Bible study he will not forget!

# Authority Over Demon Spirits

**PERSONAL NOTES**

### Number 5

LIVE IN VICTORY OVER THE DEVIL AND DEMONS BY DEPENDING UPON THE POWER OF THE INDWELLING HOLY SPIRIT.

**Isaiah 59:19**
**1 John 4:4**

### Number 6

RECOGNIZE THE IMPORTANCE OF BEING COMMITTED TO A LOCAL CHURCH AND PASTOR THAT PREACHES AND PRACTICES THE NEW TESTAMENT.

**Romans 12:1-13**
**Hebrews 10:24, 25**

You need the strength and protection of fellow Christians and godly relationships in a local church that proclaims the uncompromised Word of God and honors the Holy Spirit.

# LESSON: 10     Freedom From Demonic Influence

**KEY VERSE:**     Luke 11:20     *"But if I cast out demons with the finger of God, surely the kingdom of God has come upon you."*

**KEY TRUTH:**     The New Testament Church cast out demons and destroyed the works of the devil, and this should be the activity of the church today.

## DEMONIC INFLUENCE IN THE END TIMES

The Bible teaches that in the last days demonic activity will increase more and more because the devil knows his days are numbered.

1 Timothy 4:1

Revelation 12:11, 12

The increase of demonic activity is obvious in these last days as we see a continual wicked attack against society, such as:

- DIVORCE AND FAMILY BREAKDOWN
- CHILD ABUSE
- VIOLENCE, TERRORISM, AND CRIME ON THE INCREASE
- THE DRUG EPIDEMIC
- MURDER, RAPE, AND SERIAL KILLERS ON THE INCREASE
- THE NEW AGE DECEPTION
- UNCLEAN SPIRITS MANIFESTING – PROSTITUTION, PORNOGRAPHY, AND HOMOSEXUALITY
- THE SPIRIT OF FEAR AND CONFUSION PREVAILING IN THE NATIONS OF THE WORLD
- THE AIDS EPIDEMIC
- THE OCCULT, SATANISM, AND WITCHCRAFT EXPLOSION
- HUMANISM AND LIBERALISM IN GOVERNMENT AND EDUCATION

According to the *U. S. News and World Report*, in 1945 in public schools in the U.S.A., the seven top offenses were listed as:

(1) Talking

(2) Chewing gum

(3) Making noise

(4) Running in the halls

(5) Getting out of turn in line

(6) Wearing improper clothing

(7) Not putting paper into wastebaskets

# Freedom From Demonic Influence

**PERSONAL NOTES**

The top seven offenses listed in 1985 (40 years later, one generation):

(1) Rape

(2) Robbery

(3) Assault

(4) Burglary

(5) Arson

(6) Bombings

(7) Murder

This list is a clear revelation of how Satan and demons in the end times are increasing their diabolical attack against society at all levels.

## IMPORTANT FACTS ABOUT DEMON SPIRITS

*"We know [positively] that we are of God, and the whole world [around us] is under the power of the evil one."*

**1 John 5:19 (AMP)**

* The New Testament clearly teaches the reality and existence of the devil and demons.

  **James 4:7**

  **Mark 16:17**

* Jesus, in His earthly ministry, was continually confronting demon spirits. According to the Gospels, as much as 25% of Jesus' ministry involved casting out demon spirits in public.

  **Matthew 12:28**

  **Mark 1:32-34, 39**

* Jesus gave His disciples power and authority over all demon spirits to expose them and expel them as they went out to preach the Gospel.

  **Luke 9:1, 2**

  **Luke 10:17-19**

* The Bible records numerous incidents from the ministry of Jesus and the New Testament church where people were delivered from the power of demons as they were cast out by the spoken Word of God.

  **Mark 1:21-27**

  **Luke 7:21**

  **Mark 5:1-16**

  **Acts 16:16-18**

# Freedom From Demonic Influence

- The Bible says that Satan has a kingdom which is highly organized and operates under his command.

  Matthew 12:22-26
  Ephesians 6:12

- The Bible says that we are locked in a supernatural battle in a life and death struggle against a supernatural enemy – unseen demon forces who are trying to destroy us.

  Ephesians 6:12
  2 Corinthians 10:3-5

If you don't know your enemy and you don't know how to fight him, then you will be killed and destroyed because of your ignorance.

- The Bible tells us that Satan and demons control and manipulate people through deception, fear, and intimidation.

  2 Corinthians 11:3, 4
  2 Timothy 1:7

- Demons operate through MIND CONTROL. (2 Corinthians 4:4). They seek to influence and capture the minds of men, blinding them to the truth of the Gospel.

## TEN CHARACTERISTICS OF DEMON SPIRITS

(1)  Demons are spirits without bodies, which is why they cannot rest without being inside a body (HUMAN or ANIMAL). They need to get into a body so they can fully express their evil desires. (They begged Jesus to allow them to enter the swine).

  Ephesians 6:12
  Matthew 12:43-45

A demon is not a mental state, a habit, or a psychological condition. Rather demons are real personalities – real persons!

(2)  Demons are intelligent. They are knowledgeable about their future destiny and judgment.

  Matthew 8:28, 29

(3)  Demons have a will. They resist surrender.          Matthew 12:43-45
  Luke 8:27-33

(4)  Demons have emotions. God's Word tells us they tremble in "fear."

  James 2:19

(They fear God, they fear God's anointed Word, they fear God's anointed ministers, they fear the blood and the name of Jesus, they fear believers who know their authority in Christ.)

# Freedom From Demonic Influence

**PERSONAL NOTES**

(5) Demons have the ability to speak. They speak to people, leading them into bondages and sometimes suicide.

**Mark 1:23, 24**

(6) Demons know how strong you are in the spirit and whether or not you have power over them.

**Acts 19:13-16**

Demons recognize and obey those who have power and authority over them.

(7) Demons are restless. They roam the earth looking for bodies to enter, control, and torment.

**Matthew 12:43-45**

(8) Demons have supernatural strength.       **Mark 5:2-4**

**Acts 19:16**

They can snap chains of iron and one demon violently beat up seven men.

(9) Demons are highly organized, and like an army, they have different ranks of authority and strength.

**Ephesians 6:12**

**Matthew 12:45**

(10) Demon spirits know that Jesus Christ is God and that they must bow before and obey the NAME OF JESUS.

**Mark 1:23, 24**

**Mark 16:17**

## WHAT IS THE WORK OF DEMON SPIRITS?

(1) **Demon spirits are the cause of sickness and disease:**

- Some cause arthritis and deformities      **Luke 13:11**
- Some cause muteness of speech      **Matthew 9:33**
- Some cause epilepsy      **Matthew 17:15-18**
- Some cause deafness      **Mark 9:25**
- Some cause blindness      **Matthew 12:22**
- Some cause physical injuries      **Mark 9:18**
- Some cause fever      **Luke 4:39**

(2) **Demon spirits cause mental oppression, depression, and insanity.**

**Isaiah 61:3**

**Matthew 8:28**

**Mark 5:1-15**

# Freedom From Demonic Influence

- There are demons of insanity.
- There are demons of heaviness and depression.

Acts 10:38

(3) Demon spirits teach and propagate false doctrine, false cults, and false prophets.

1 Timothy 4:1

(4) Demon spirits blind the minds of unbelievers, preventing them from seeing the truth of the Gospel.

2 Corinthians 4:4
Acts 26:18

- There are MIND BLINDING DEMONS OF MIND CONTROL.

(5) Demon spirits entice and seduce people into all kinds of sin, deception, heresies, and false religions.

Mark 13:22
1 John 2:26
2 Corinthians 11:3
1 Timothy 4:1,2

- Seducing spirits are out to tempt, corrupt, and lead you astray.

(6) Demon spirits oppress and drive people to suicide.

Matthew 17:15
Mark 9:20-22
John 10:10

(7) The Bible speaks of lying spirits, familiar spirits, and spirits of divination that draw people and attract them into the bondage of witchcraft, sorcery, and the occult.

2 Chronicles 33:1-6
2 Thessalonians 2:9-12
Acts 8:9
Acts 16:16
Revelation 9:20, 21

(8) Demon spirits bind and afflict people with all kinds of physical pain and maladies.

Matthew 12:22
Luke 13:11- 16
Matthew 4:23, 24

# Freedom From Demonic Influence

(9)     Demon spirits torment people with the bondage of fear and phobias of every kind.

> Romans 8:15
> 2 Timothy 1:7
> 1 John 4:18

(10)    Demon spirits, called familiar spirits in the Bible, imitate the departed dead, snaring people in a web of deception.

> Leviticus 20:6, 27
> 1 Samuel 28:3-9

  • Spiritualistic mediums, seances, and psychics operate through familiar spirits (demons).

(11)    Demon spirits wage spiritual warfare against the church, ministers of the Gospel, and the work of God.

> Matthew 16:18, 19
> 1 Thessalonians 2:18
> Matthew 13:19
> 2 Corinthians 10:3-5
> Ephesians 6:10-13

(12)    Demon spirits seek embodiment in human beings and they can go out of and come back into men as they will, unless cast out and rejected.

> Matthew 12:43-45

(13)    Demons are restless and they produce restlessness in the people they control.

> Matthew 12:43
> Isaiah 57:20, 21

## HOW DO DEMONS GAIN ENTRY INTO PEOPLE'S LIVES?

John 8:34              Ephesians 4:27              Romans 6:16

There are a number of ways people open the door for Satanic attack, giving demon spirits legal ground for entry into their lives.

### Number 1

Demons can enter through drugs and alcohol.

> 1 Corinthians 10:21
> Proverbs 23:29-33

Drugs and alcohol make a person highly susceptible to demons because they are not in control of their minds. Their minds become an open doorway for demons to enter.

# Freedom From Demonic Influence

## Number 2

Demons can enter through any type of involvement with the occult.

**Deuteronomy 18:9-12**

Any contact, involvement with, or practice in the occult, by yourself or your parents, is a doorway for demons to enter and influence your life.

This includes contact or practice with the following:

- Fortune telling
- Numerology
- Palmistry
- Tarot cards
- Ouija board
- Spiritualism, attending seances or attempting to communicate with the spirits of the departed dead
- Astrology
- Mind control or mind dynamics
- Faith healing
- Astral projection
- Belief in reincarnation
- Witchcraft
- Sorcery
- Satanism and demon worship
- Handwriting analysis
- Karate and all martial arts

- Reading horoscopes
- Tea leaf reading
- Crystal ball gazing
- Playing occult games such as dungeons and dragons
- Hypnotism
- Automatic writing
- Black or white magic
- E.S.P.
- Telepathy
- Psychic healing
- Using or wearing charms
- Yoga exercises
- Belief in any Hindu doctrines or Eastern philosophies.
- Star signs (zodiac)
- T. M. (transcendental meditation)
- Hard rock music or heavy metal music

- Having occult books or objects in your home, e. g. Buddha figures, books on U.F.O.'s, magic, eastern mysticism, etc.

*"Nor shall you bring an abomination into your house, lest you be doomed to destruction like it. You shall utterly detest it and utterly abhor it, for it is an accursed thing."*

**Deuteronomy 7:26**

*"Give no regard to mediums and familiar spirits; do not seek after them, to be defiled by them: I am the Lord your God."*

**Leviticus 19:31**

- This comes about through visiting or making contact with fortune tellers,

# Freedom From Demonic Influence

© 1994 The Believer's School of Training, Rev. Norman K. Robertson

**PERSONAL NOTES**

gypsies, witches, spiritualist mediums, psychics, hypnotists, witchdoctors, or demonic places of worship, e. g. Hindu temples, etc.

- All involvement with the occult must be repented of, renounced, and the curse broken in your life.

## Number 3

Demons can enter children if their parents worshiped pagan gods, or were involved in Satanism or the occult.

**Exodus 20:1-5**

- Dedicating children to Satan or sexual abuse (incest) of children brings demonic strongholds.

- All idol worship is demonic.

**Psalm 106:35-37**

## Number 4

Demons can enter people's lives through repeated acts of sin, yielding to the lusts of the flesh, practicing unclean habits.

**1 Corinthians 6:9-20**

e.g. sexual immorality, adultery, fornication, pornography, homosexuality, or any kind of sexual perversion.

- Demons capitalize on the works of the flesh.

- Demon spirits have entry points into our lives if we sin with our body and live in rebellion against God and His Word. Sowing to the flesh means we will reap corruption.

*"Do not be deceived, God is not mocked; for whatever a man sows, that he will also reap. For he who sows to his flesh will of the flesh reap corruption, but he who sows to the Spirit will of the Spirit reap everlasting life."*

**Galatians 6:7, 8**

## Number 5

Demons can enter through a person's thought life.        **2 Timothy 1:7**

For example:
- A mind that has turned against God.
- A mind open to all kinds of fantasies.
- A mind that yields to fear and depression – suicidal thoughts, lustful thoughts of adultery, etc.

# Freedom From Demonic Influence

## Number 6

Demons can enter through unforgiveness, bitterness or hatred in our lives. Persistent bad attitudes can become strongholds.

**Matthew 18:21-35**

## Number 7

Demons can enter through transference.

(1) submitting to or being influenced by people who are not Christians.

(2) movies, television, and videos that are full of fear, horror, violence, and sexual lust.

(3) books and magazines.

(4) through sexual intercourse, rape, incest, and homosexuality. Most homosexuals began as children who were molested.

## Number 8

Demons can enter through people following false religions, heresies, and cults.

**1 John 4:1-3**
**1 Timothy 4:1, 2**

- Seducing spirits of deception preach false doctrines and draw millions of people into error and spiritual bondage.

Examples of false religion:

- THE MORMONS
- JEHOVAH WITNESSES
- SPIRITUALISM
- HARE KRISHNA
- BUDDHISM
- SCIENTOLOGY
- ALL EASTERN PHILOSOPHIES AND RELIGIONS

- CHRISTIAN SCIENCE
- NEW AGE MOVEMENT
- SECRET SOCIETIES, (such as Freemasonry)
- HINDUISM
- ISLAM
- CHRISTADELPHIANS, etc.
- WORLDWIDE CHURCH OF GOD (Herbert W. Armstrong)

**KEY TRUTH:** BEHIND EVERY FALSE RELIGION, FALSE PROPHET, FALSE DOCTRINE, AND FALSE CULT IS A DEMON SPIRIT.

## CAN A CHRISTIAN HAVE A DEMON?

Is there a difference between possession and influence? Yes!

The born-again Christian CANNOT BE DEMON POSSESSED, but can be troubled, oppressed, or influenced by the action of evil spirits.

# Freedom From Demonic Influence

© 1994 The Believer's School of Training, Rev. Norman K. Robertson

**PERSONAL NOTES**

(1) **Demonic possession means** a complete takeover and ownership of spirit, soul, and body. Evil spirits indwell, occupy, and control the person's personality. ONLY LOST PEOPLE CAN BE POSSESSED BY DEMONS.

**Examples of demon possession** (Evil spirits indwelling and totally controlling people):

• People who commit rape, murder, child abuse, e.g. serial killers. They are **PSYCHOPATHS.** They manifest extreme cruelty.

• The **SCHIZOPHRENIC** is a person who withdraws from reality and loses contact with reality.

• People who are **PARANOID** have delusions of being somebody else. They are unable to accept themselves as they really are, but imagine themselves to be Napoleon, or some film star, or a war hero, etc. They live in a fantasy world and can be controlled by all types of unnatural fears.

• The **MANIC DEPRESSIVE** has severe ups and downs, severe feelings of rejection, and destructive behavior–suicidal tendencies.

(2) **Demonic influence means** that there are specific areas in a person's life (CHRISTIAN or NON-CHRISTIAN) where demon spirits attack, afflict, oppress, torment, or hold in bondage and occupy.

**Examples:**

• THE MIND – FEAR; CONFUSION; INSANITY; FILTHY, UNCLEAN THOUGHTS.
• THE TONGUE – CONSTANT LYING; UNCLEAN SPEECH; BLASPHEMY; CRITICISM.
• SEX – LUST; ADULTERY; HOMOSEXUALITY; LESBIANISM; PORNOGRAPHY.
• UNCLEAN HABITS AND ADDICTIONS – ALCOHOL; HOOKED ON DIETING; SMOKING; FOODAHOLIC; USE OF DRUGS; HOOKED ON ROCK MUSIC; ETC.
• PHYSICAL SICKNESS – EPILEPSY; FITS; ASTHMA; MIGRAINES; DEAFNESS; ARTHRITIS; ALLERGIES; CANCER; ETC.
• EMOTIONS AND ATTITUDES – UNNATURAL RESTLESSNESS; REJECTION; HATRED; ENVY; ANGER; BITTERNESS; TENSION; JEALOUSY; SELF-PITY; DEPRESSION; RESENTMENT; HEAVINESS; DESPAIR; SUICIDE.

Christians cannot be demon-possessed but they can be troubled by demons and attacked with demonic oppression. They can be influenced and held in demonic bondage in their body or soul (MIND, WILL, EMOTIONS), but NOT in their re-created spirit.

A Christian who sincerely seeks to live for God (Romans 12:1, 2) and attempts to live a disciplined lifestyle (prayer, attending church, reading the Bible, walking upright before the Lord), yet has recurrent or persistent problem areas in their life that they cannot control, needs to be set free from demon spirits.

A child of God living outside the will of God in rebellion or disobedience to the commands of the Scripture is an OPEN TARGET for demon spirits.

# Freedom From Demonic Influence

© *1994 The Believer's School of Training, Rev. Norman K. Robertson*

- Christians can have demons. They can be demonized or troubled by demons.

- Christians are the target of demonic attack and activity.

- Christians cannot be demon-possessed.

- Demon possession means total ownership and being indwelt and ruled by evil spirits – spirit, soul, and body.

Bible examples of believers being demonized:

(1) KING SAUL went from serving God into witchcraft.

(2) THE DAUGHTER OF ABRAHAM afflicted with a spirit of infirmity for eighteen years in Luke 13.

(3) JUDAS ISCARIOT yielded to Satan, stole money, betrayed Jesus, and later committed suicide.

(4) The case of ANANIAS AND SAPPHIRA in Acts 5.

(5) The case of the BELIEVER IN CORINTH who was committing incest.

There is a process of being demonized.                    **Matthew 12:43-45**

Living in disobedience to God means we are living outside of God's will for our lives, and that means we are living outside of God's protection!

- There is a **POINT OF CONTACT**. Through our eyes, ears, mind, or body we give demons legal ground to influence and work in our lives.

- There is a **PATHWAY OF ENTRY**. Repeated acts of sin, habitual yielding to the flesh in certain areas, or practicing unclean habits, opens us to demons entering and oppressing areas of our lives.

- There is an **INWARD HOLD** where demons have come into a person's life and occupy and control areas of their life.

This is where demons have to be cast out.                    **Mark 16:17**

## HOW DO WE RECOGNIZE DEMON ACTIVITY?

There are tell-tale symptoms present in peoples' lives who are "DEMONIZED." This means they are being influenced by, tormented, and oppressed by DEMONS or, in some cases, they are demon-possessed.

This list is incomplete but can help you to identify demonic problems:

(1) Living in bondage to fear, depression, anxiety, anger, or rage.

(2) An addiction to drugs, tobacco or alcohol, and attempts to break these habits have been unsuccessful. Chain smokers are prisoners of demons.

# Freedom From Demonic Influence

**PERSONAL NOTES**

(3) Being in bondage to sinful attitudes like self-hatred, unforgiveness, bitterness, resentment, and hate.

(4) Involvement with the occult (the occult is the devil's supernatural) either in the present or past.

(5) Chronic physical sickness, especially sicknesses that have been in the family for several generations, e. g. deafness, cancer, heart problems, arthritis, etc.

(6) Contorted physical reactions when the Holy Spirit is present such as in a worship service, or in a prayer meeting, or the preaching of God's Word.

(7) A disturbed family history which may have involved rejection, incest, rape, alcoholism, and various forms of child abuse.

(8) Uncontrollable compulsive desires that hold you in bondage, such as eating disorders (Anorexia/Bulimia), lust, fornication, pornography, homosexuality, stealing, lying, or suicide.

## HOW TO BE FREE FROM DEMON SPIRITS

The rule is simple. ANY AREA of your life or behavior that is out of control, that is compulsive, that is obsessive, that is not under the control of Jesus, is under the influence and in bondage to demon spirits.

*"Therefore if the Son makes you free, you shall be free indeed."*

**John 8:36**

(1) Come to Jesus Christ and admit your need to be free.

(2) Ask God to forgive you, renounce and repent of all known sin (e.g. Adultery, Homosexuality, Rock Music, Pornography, etc.)

(3) Forgive every person that has ever wronged you or hurt you in some way. Otherwise, unforgiveness will be a blockage to your deliverance.

(4) Receive cleansing and forgiveness through the Blood of Jesus.

(5) Call upon the name of Jesus for your deliverance and command the spirits oppressing your life to leave you NOW IN JESUS' NAME. "DEMONS OUT, IN JESUS' NAME."

(6) Stay delivered by living under the Lordship of Jesus and giving the devil no place in your life.

This involves:

Daily prayer and Bible study
Faithful church attendance
Staying filled with the Holy Spirit
Resisting the devil and temptation with:
(1) The spoken Word of God
(2) The Blood of Jesus
(3) The name of Jesus

**IMPORTANT:** *Set aside 15 minutes each day to read and review these study notes until your mind is renewed to the victory and dominion you have in Christ over the devil and all demons.*

## KEY QUESTIONS

(1) Did God create Satan and demons? Explain.

(2) How can we discern the difference between the flesh controlling our lives or demonic forces?

(3) What is the difference between demons and fallen angels?

(4) Give four activities of the work of demon spirits today.

(5) Can a Christian have a demon? Explain with Scriptures.

(6) What are the signs of increased demon activity in the last days?

## MEMORY WORK

Luke 9:1, 2

Mark 16:17

Luke 11:20

## PERSONAL APPLICATION

(1) Are there any areas of your life where you are giving Satan and demons a foothold? If so, will you now repent and get free?

(2) Take your Bible concordance and look up all the New Testament verses on Satan and demons.

(3) When was the last time you ministered to someone needing deliverance? What happened?

(4) Do you know how to take the Word of God and set people free who are living in bondage?

## RECOMMENDED READING:

Norvel Hayes, *Know Your Enemy*

Lester Sumrall, *Exorcism*

Kenneth E. Hagin, *The Triumphant Church*

Rick Godwin, *Training for Reigning*

# LESSON: 11                                                          Casting Out Demons

**KEY VERSE:**    Luke 10:17, 19      *"Then the seventy returned with joy, saying, 'Lord, even the demons are subject to us in Your name...'*

*Behold, I give you the authority to trample on serpents and scorpions, and over all the power of the enemy, and nothing shall by any means hurt you."*

**KEY TRUTH:**    So often, many in the church are afraid of demons because they do not know about their legal defeat at Calvary and the believer's position of authority over them IN JESUS' NAME.

## THE ORIGIN OF DEMON SPIRITS

There is some confusion about this in the church, yet Scripture is very clear:

(1) Demons are not the spirits of the departed dead.

(2) Demons are not the fallen angels who fell with Satan in his rebellion against Heaven.

There is a distinct difference between fallen angels and demons in Scripture.

Angels have wings and demons do not have wings.

**Daniel 9:21**

Angels inhabit the heavenlies, while demon spirits are earth bound.

**Ephesians 2:2**
**Ephesians 6:12**
**Matthew 12:43**
**Mark 5:1-13**

Angels have bodies of their own and do not desire to occupy another body, while demons have an intense craving to enter and inhabit a body, either a human body or that of an animal.

**Matthew 12:43-45**
**Mark 5:11-13**

Demons prefer the body of a man, so they can gratify their evil desires and perversion.

(3) Demons are the disembodied spirit beings of the PRE-ADAMIC RACE.

• They are called in Scripture, evil spirits, unclean spirits, and demons.

• They are real personalities, able to think, act, and speak.

# Casting Out Demons

**PERSONAL NOTES**

**What the New Testament church understood about the devil and demon spirits.**

(1) They knew and believed in the existence of Satan and demon spirits.

**Acts 5:3, 16**
**Acts 26:18**

(2) They understood that the purpose of the devil is to steal, kill, and destroy.

**2 Corinthians 2:11**
**John 10:10**

(3) They knew that demon spirits deceived, oppressed, and possessed men.

**Acts 16:16**

(4) They recognized that they were involved in spiritual warfare and the real enemy was not physical ,or flesh and blood, but invisible evil forces, persons without bodies.

**Ephesians 6:10-13**

(5) They knew that demons recognize and obey those who have power over them IN JESUS' NAME.

**Luke 10:17-20**
**Acts 19:13-16**

(6) They understood that every lost person who blinds their mind to the truth of the Gospel, is under the influence and control of demon spirits.

**Acts 26:18**
**2 Corinthians 4:4**
**Ephesians 2:1-3**

(7) They knew that the devil and demons are the source of sickness and disease.

**Acts 10:38**

Disease is Satan's attack on our bodies.

(8) They knew their authority, IN JESUS' NAME, to resist the devil and cast out demons.

**Mark 16:17**
**Acts 16:18**
**James 4:7**

## FIVE ASPECTS OF DEMONIC ACTIVITY

(1) Demons want to enslave you with addictions and uncontrollable compulsive desires, such as drugs, alcoholism, sexual perversion, smoking, and food addictions.

**Romans 8:15**
**John 8:34**

# Casting Out Demons

(2) Demons want to delude and deceive you with false doctrines, false religions, and a counterfeit Gospel.

**1 Timothy 4:1, 2**

Demons can present themselves as angels of light, promoting a false Jesus, a false Gospel, and counterfeit GIFTS of the Spirit.

A seducing demon of DECEPTION is behind every false teaching, false religion, false cult and philosophy being promoted in the world today.

(3) Demon spirits are the source of sickness and disease.

**Acts 10:38**

(4) Demons harass and torment people with fear, depression, and oppression.

**2 Timothy 1:7**

**1 John 4:18**

Satan is behind any type of fear, vexation, insomnia, or tormenting thought.

(5) Demons wage warfare against the church of God, attacking, hindering, and opposing believers every way they can.

**Ephesians 6:10-18**

They will attack our minds, bodies, finances, families, and relationships with people. They try to hinder us from living for God and doing the works of Jesus.

The devil and demons are terrified of being exposed and expelled.

*"You are of God, little children, and have overcome them, because He who is in you is greater than he who is in the world."*

**1 John 4:4**

Three things Satan and demons hate and fear:

(1) The spoken Word of God

(2) The authority of the name of Jesus

(3) The Blood of the cross

God's Word does not tell us to interview and hold discussions with demons. We are to bind them and cast them out.

## HOW DID JESUS DEAL WITH DEMONIZED PEOPLE?

The ministry of Jesus touched the three great areas of human need: sin, sickness and bondage to evil spirits.

Therefore, Jesus' commission to the church includes all three. We are to preach the Gospel, heal the sick, and cast out demons.

# Casting Out Demons

## TEN WAYS JESUS DEALT WITH DEMON SPIRITS

(1) Twenty-five percent of the ministry of Jesus was dedicated to exposing and expelling demon spirits. Deliverance was a normal part of His ministry.

**Mark 1:39**

**Luke 7:21**

(2) Jesus dealt with demonized people in public and cast the demons out publicly.

**Luke 4:33-36, 40, 41**

(3) Often, when Jesus commanded the demons to come out, there were powerful physical manifestations.

**Mark 1:26**

**Mark 9:20**

(4) Jesus did not counsel or interview demons all night. He commanded them to come out, and they did so immediately.

**Matthew 8:16, 28-32**

(5) Sometimes, during deliverance, Jesus laid hands on people. At other times, He cast spirits out with a command of faith.

**Luke 4:40, 41**

**Matthew 8:16**

(6) In Bible days, parents were responsible for bringing their children to Jesus for deliverance.

**Mark 9:21-25**

**Matthew 15:22-28**

Notice here that Jesus required faith on the part of the parents for the child to be set free.

(7) Jesus cast out demons by the power and anointing of the Holy Spirit.

**Matthew 12:28**

**Luke 11:20**

(8) When Jesus cast out demons, He never commanded them to go into Hell or into the pit.

**Mark 1:25, 26**

**Mark 9:25**

Jesus knew that God has a time ordained when Satan and all evil spirits will be bound and punished.

**Revelation 20:3, 10**

(9) Jesus encouraged those who had been delivered to testify of their deliverance.

**Mark 5:18-20**

**Luke 8:1, 2**

# Casting Out Demons

**(10)** Jesus never sent any of His disciples out to preach the Gospel without commissioning them to cast out demon spirits.

Matthew 10:1

Luke 9:1

Mark 16:17

## FIVE THINGS THE BELIEVER MUST KNOW TO WIN IN SPIRITUAL WARFARE

*"This charge I commit to you, son Timothy, according to the prophecies previously made concerning you, that by them you may wage the good warfare."*

1 Timothy 1:18

### Number 1

Know exactly who your real enemy is – the devil and demon spirits.

**Ephesians 6:12**

### Number 2

Know the strategies, devices, and operations of the devil coming against you, your family, and your community.

**2 Corinthians 2:11**

### Number 3

Know you already have the victory over the devil and demons because Jesus conquered them at Calvary.

**Colossians 2:15**

### Number 4

Know that the devil and all demon spirits are subject to you and must bow to the name of Jesus.

**Luke 10:17-20**

### Number 5

Know all of the weapons that God has given you and use them boldly against the enemy and his attacks.

**Ephesians 6:10-18**

# Casting Out Demons

**PERSONAL NOTES**

## DIVINE WEAPONS OF WARFARE

### WHAT WEAPONS HAS GOD GIVEN THE CHURCH TO CONFRONT AND COMBAT EVIL SPIRITS?

2 Corinthians 10:3-5
Ephesians 6:10-18

| | | |
|---|---|---|
| (1) | The Blood of Jesus | Revelation 12:11 |
| (2) | The spoken Word of God | Hebrews 4:12 |
| (3) | The name of Jesus | Philippians 2:9-11 |
| (4) | The weapons of prayer, fasting, and intercession | Isaiah 58:6, Ephesians 6:18 |
| (5) | The operation of the gifts of the Spirit | 1 Corinthians 12:7-11 |
| (6) | The power of praying in tongues | Romans 8:26, 27 |
| (7) | The anointing of the Holy Spirit | Isaiah 10:27 |
| (8) | The power of binding and loosing | Matthew 18:18 |
| (9) | The weapon of praise and worship | Isaiah 61:3, Psalm 149:6-9 |
| (10) | The whole armor of God | Ephesians 6:10-18 |

*"So shall they fear the name of the Lord from the west, And His glory from the rising of the sun; When the enemy comes in, like a flood, The Spirit of the Lord will lift up a standard against him."*

**Isaiah 59:19**

# LESSON: 12      Setting The Captives Free

**KEY VERSE:**      James 4:7      *"Therefore submit to God. Resist the devil and he will flee from you."*

**KEY TRUTH:**      We must be seekers and applicators of God's truth — hearing is incomplete in itself without doing.

Now that we have a scriptural foundation about our authority over Satan and demons, we must exercise it boldly, in Jesus' name, and set the captives free.

*"And these signs will follow those who believe: In my name they will cast out demons; they will speak with new tongues; They will take up serpents; and if they drink anything deadly, it will by no means hurt them; they will lay hands on the sick, and they will recover."*

         **Mark 16:17, 18**

Every Christian should have the supernatural sign of casting out demons.

All believers should demonstrate their authority in Christ and cast out demons.

Demon forces and evil spirits are real!

The Bible talks about:

* Demon spirits of oppression and fear
* Spirits of infirmity
* Spirits of insanity
* Deaf and dumb spirits
* Unclean spirits
* Spirits of blindness

<u>Fact Number 1:</u>      RECOGNIZE SATAN AND DEMON SPIRITS AS THE REAL ENEMY OF THE HUMAN RACE, AND NOT GOD.

*"How God anointed Jesus of Nazareth with the Holy Spirit and with power, who went about doing good and healing all who were oppressed by the devil, for God was with Him."*

         **Acts 10:38**

*"Put on the whole armor of God, that you may be able to stand against the wiles of the devil. For we do not wrestle against flesh and blood, but against principalities, against powers, against the rulers of the darkness of this age, against spiritual hosts of wickedness in the heavenly places."*

         **Ephesians 6:11, 12**

# Setting The Captives Free

**PERSONAL NOTES**

*"Be sober, be vigilant; because your adversary the devil walks about like a roaring lion, seeking whom he may devour."*

**1 Peter 5:8**

*"The thief does not come except to steal, and to kill, and to destroy. I have come that they may have life, and that they may have it more abundantly.*

**John 10:10**

Read and study Job, Chapters 1 and 2.

*"Therefore submit to God. Resist the devil and he will flee from you."*

**James 4:7**

The source of sickness, disease, tragedy, calamity, oppression, fear, and trouble is Satan and demon spirits! God is good and God is love. Stop blaming Him for everything the devil does. Psalm 23 is a revelation of the true character of God.

<u>Fact Number 2:</u>   **GET THE BIBLE REVELATION IN YOUR SPIRIT, THAT SATAN AND ALL DEMONS ARE ETERNALLY DEFEATED.**

Read Luke 11:14-22

Jesus identifies Satan as the strong man and then He described, step by step, what He would do to Satan by the work of Calvary.

*"When a strong man, fully armed, guards his own palace, his goods are in peace. But when a stronger than he comes upon him and overcomes him, he takes from him all his armor in which he trusted, and divides his spoils."*

**Luke 11:21, 22**

(1) The stronger one (Jesus Christ) would come upon Satan.

(2) The stronger one (Jesus Christ) would overcome Satan.

(3) The stronger one (Jesus Christ) would take away all Satan's armor (strip away all his power).

(4) The stronger one (Jesus Christ) would divide his spoils.

These four things describe Jesus' conquest over Satan!

Jesus came upon him, He overcame him, He stripped him of all authority, and He divided his spoils with us!

*"[God] disarmed the principalities and powers that were ranged against us and made a bold display and public example of them, in triumphing over them in Him and in it [the cross]."*

**Colossians 2:15 (AMP)**

# Setting The Captives Free

*"Inasmuch then as the children have partaken of flesh and blood, He Himself likewise shared in the same, that through death He might destroy him who had the power of death, that is, the devil, and release those who through fear of death were all their lifetime subject to bondage."*

Hebrews 2:14, 15

*". . .For this purpose the Son of God was manifested, that He might destroy the works of the devil."*

1 John 3:8

*"I am He who lives, and was dead, and behold, I am alive for evermore. Amen. And I have the keys of Hades and of Death."*

Revelation 1:18

Jesus said, "In My Name all believers should exercise the same authority I have and cast out demon forces."

As believers in Christ, none of us should be tormented by demons or be in need of deliverance from evil spirits. BUT, we should live free from demons and be out in the world bringing deliverance to suffering humanity!

**Fact Number 3:**  JESUS GAVE US POWER AND AUTHORITY TO USE HIS NAME TO CAST OUT DEMONS AND ENFORCE SATAN'S DEFEAT.

*"When evening had come, they brought to Him many who were demon-possessed. And He cast out the spirits with a word, and healed all who were sick."*

Matthew 8:16

*"Then He called His twelve disciples together and gave them power and authority over all demons, and to cure diseases."*

Luke 9:1

**KEY TRUTH:**  REALIZE THE DIVINE AUTHORITY YOU HAVE IN CHRIST AND IN THE SPIRIT WORLD. WE HAVE POWER OVER ALL DEMONS.

*"Then the seventy returned with joy, saying, Lord, even the demons are subject to us in your name."*

Luke 10:17

# Setting The Captives Free

© 1994 The Believer's School of Training, Rev. Norman K. Robertson

**PERSONAL NOTES**

*"Behold, I give you the authority to trample on serpents and scorpions, and over all the power of the enemy, and nothing shall by any means hurt you. Nevertheless do not rejoice in this, that the spirits are subject to you, but rather rejoice because your names are written in heaven."*

Luke 10:19, 20

*"And these signs will follow those who believe: In My name they will cast out demons; they will speak with new tongues."*

Mark 16:17

*"Therefore submit to God. Resist the devil and he will flee from you."*

James 4:7

*"I will not talk with you much more, for the prince (evil genius, ruler) of the world is coming. And he has no claim on Me - he has nothing in common with Me, there is nothing in Me that belongs to him, he has no power over Me."*

John 14:30 (AMP)

* Child of God, always picture yourself as a TOTAL CONQUEROR!

* You have divine dominion over Satan and over all evil spirits!

* You have the authority, in Christ, to break Satan's power over the lives of people around you and free the captives.

* You have the spiritual weapons of the Blood of Jesus, the Word of God, the name of Jesus, and the power of the Holy Spirit to demonstrate Satan's defeat and walk in absolute victory.

## HOW TO IDENTIFY AND DISCERN DEMONIC INFLUENCE

The Bible teaches that demon spirits are real and they can invade, enter, and inhabit areas of our lives. All Christians, and even dedicated, radical Christians, including ministers, are targets for Satan and demonic attack.

Any area of your life that is not FULLY SURRENDERED to Jesus and His Lordship is open to the influence, oppression, and activity of demon spirits.

* Any area of your life that is compulsive

* Any part of your life where you feel driven

* Any area of your life which is obsessive or out of control reveals the presence and activity of demon spirits at work.

# Setting The Captives Free

For instance:

- maybe you have an unnatural fear controlling your life. (Fear of failure, fear of rejection, fear of sickness and disease, fear of poverty, fear of old age, fear of being alone, etc.)

- or else you have depression and a spirit of heaviness that hangs over your life like a cloud controlling you. It seems unbreakable.

- or, perhaps your life is consumed with hatred, with deep seated bitterness, with anger, with thoughts of resentment and revenge – you must "get even" no matter what the cost.

- or, perhaps compulsive worry and anxiety oppresses your mind day after day. You have an inability to cope with the pressures of life, or you can't think straight and you are all confused.

- maybe a sense of rejection and insecurity dogs your life.

- or else you have mood swings and emotions that are constantly up and down – you are restless. Restlessness is a key character trait of evil spirits.

- perhaps you have thought patterns of suicide that bombard your mind until you feel like ending your life. Remember, Jesus said that Satan is a murderer!

*"When an unclean spirit goes out of a man, he goes through dry places, seeking rest, and finds none."*

Matthew 12:43

*"But the wicked are like the troubled sea, When it cannot rest, Whose waters cast up mire and dirt. 'There is no peace,' Says my God, 'for the wicked.'"*

Isaiah 57:20, 21

## TELL-TALE SIGNS OF DEMONIC ACTIVITY

(1) **Demonic activity in the speech area**
   Demon spirits can be behind lying, unclean talk, blasphemy, bad language, gossip, slander, sowing strife and discord with your tongue, a critical tongue.

(2) **Demonic activity through addiction**
   Anything that drives you, compels you, and controls you is not from God, but is an evil spirit out to destroy you – drugs, alcohol, smoking, anorexia, food addictions, being hooked on diets, pills, tranquilizers, pain killers, or some medication.

(3) **Demonic activity in the thought life**
   Uncontrollable impure, unclean thoughts, fear, depression, rejection, doubt, compulsive worry and anxiety, self-hatred, indecision, confusion, procrastination, thoughts of perversion, sexual lust and fantasizing, extreme moodiness, violent thoughts of envy, jealousy, revenge, hatred, and suicide. Unbelief is a spirit which is ANTI-CHRIST and ANTI-GOD and ANTI-BIBLE.

# Setting The Captives Free

**PERSONAL NOTES**

**(4) Demonic activity in the sexual area**

If you are "driven" to commit fornication, adultery, perverted sex, or homosexuality, then you are being controlled by a demon of lust. If you have a passion for pornography (videos and magazines, etc.), perversion, and your mind is filled with unclean desires, then you are under the INFLUENCE of UNCLEAN SPIRITS.

- Sex in the marriage relationship is good, holy, and pure.
- Perversion, homosexuality, and extra-marital affairs are UNHOLY, IMPURE, and an ABOMINATION to God.

**(5) Demonic activity and oppression in the physical body**

If you have suffered with chronic sickness for years or else you have hereditary illness in your body, then it is the work of demons.

Physical infirmities such as allergies, arthritis, cancer, tumors, blindness, deafness, epilepsy, asthma, migraine, paralysis, etc. are often caused by demon spirits.

**Acts 10:38**
**Acts 19:11, 12**
**Luke 13:11**

These Scriptures associate evil spirits and sickness together.
Also, things like insomnia, sleeplessness, and restlessness are demonic.

**(6) Demonic activity in the realm of the spirit**

Demons control people who are engaged in all occult activities such as ouija boards, horoscopes, fortune-telling, palmistry, the use of crystals, tea leaf reading, dungeons and dragons and other occultic games, mind control, spiritualism, attempting to contact or consult the dead, witchcraft, sorcery, Satanism, yoga and practicing martial arts, videos or movies that promote the demonic, witches, wizards and spells.

Acid rock music and heavy metal music are demonic and occultic.
The lyrics promote rebellion, violence, rape, incest, drug abuse, suicide, and Satanism, etc., perverting the minds and putting young people into every kind of bondage.

## HOW TO BE SET FREE AND LIVE FREE FROM DEMONIC OPPRESSION

*"Stand fast therefore in the liberty by which Christ has made us free, and do not be entangled again with a yoke of bondage."*

**Galatians 5:1**

## Number 1

**Humble yourself before God and be committed to living a pure, holy life under the Lordship of Jesus.**

**1 Peter 5:6-9**
**1 John 5:18**

# Setting The Captives Free

Put all unconfessed sin and fleshly compromise out of your life.

## Number 2
**Realize who you are IN CHRIST and put on the whole armor of God.**

Ephesians 6:10-18

- The devil and demons are under your feet.
- All demon spirits are subject to you IN JESUS' NAME.
- Protect your spiritual life and heart with all diligence.
- Keep yourself full of God – His Word and His Spirit.

## Number 3
**Shut the door on the devil and give him no place or foothold in your life.**

Ephesians 4:26, 27

How do we open the door to Satan?

- By negative thinking or speaking negatively (watch your words).
- By watching movies, videos, or T. V. programs that promote sin, fear, lust, violence, adultery, the works of the flesh, etc.
- By reading ungodly books and magazines that promote the works of the flesh.
- By going to places of temptation (devil's territory) where Christians should not go, e.g. nightclubs, disco's, casinos, X-Rated movie houses, bars, etc.

Stay Off the devil's Territory.

The Bible says, "Abstain from all appearance of evil."
- By having ungodly relationships or unsaved friends.
- By committing illicit sex (living together), drinking alcohol, or taking drugs.
- By neglect of your spiritual life – not reading your Bible and praying every day, inconsistent church attendance.

## Number 4
**Be filled with the Spirit, walk in the Spirit, pray in the Spirit, and live in the Spirit.**

1 John 4:4
Ephesians 5:18
Galatians 5:16
Jude 20

Living a Spirit-controlled life is essential to overcoming demon powers. This means

# Setting The Captives Free

**PERSONAL NOTES**

yielding every part of your life to the Lordship of Christ.

There is one baptism in the Holy Spirit but there are many RE-FILLINGS, REFRESHINGS, and repeated renewals of the Spirit. "Be continually filled with the Holy Spirit."

## Number 5

**Resist the devil and his devices with the overcoming weapons of the Blood, the Word of God, and the name of Jesus.**

> 2 Corinthians 2:11
> James 4:7
> Revelation 12:11

Don't allow the enemy for ONE MINUTE to make you sick, fearful, depressed, or get you into sin.

## Number 6

**Live under the spiritual protection of a strong local church and develop godly friendships with spirit filled Christians who will build you up, encourage you, and pray with you.**

> Ephesians 4:11, 12
> Hebrews 10:24, 25
> Hebrews 13:17

Join a New Testament church (Mark 16).

* Be committed and get involved in the vision of your local church.
* Submit to the authority of your pastor and be a blessing to the local church.
* Get involved in church activities along with fellow members of the congregation.

## HOW TO MINISTER DELIVERANCE
### Luke 4:18          Mark 16:17

In preparing to minister to demonized people:

Remember, your position in Jesus Christ is one of power, authority, and dominion.

* At Calvary, Jesus conquered the devil and all demon spirits (Colossians 2:15). Your enemy is already defeated and under your feet.

* After His Resurrection, Jesus gave every believer the power of His name and authority over all demon spirits. All demons are subject to you IN JESUS' NAME. (Luke 10:17)

* The Holy Spirit in you is much more powerful than any devil or demon forces. (1 John 4:4)

# Setting The Captives Free

**Setting the captives free. . .practical instructions**

(1)   Don't be afraid or allow the fear of demons to attack you when praying for people's deliverance. Be bold and know your authority IN CHRIST.

**2 Timothy 1:7**

DEMONS UNDERSTAND AUTHORITY!

(2)   Ask the Holy Spirit to anoint you for ministry and trust the Holy Spirit for His Gifts to operate — words of knowledge and discerning of spirits enable you to identify demons influencing people.

**Luke 11:13**
**Matthew 12:28**

(3)   Make a correct diagnosis. Locate the person by asking questions before you pray.

**1 John 4:1-3**

Ask:

Have you renounced and repented of all sin in your life?

Have you made Jesus Lord in every part of your life?

Do you really want to be set free from this bondage?

Do you believe that Jesus Christ is the Son of God and that through His Blood and in His name you can be delivered now?

Remember, for a person to be delivered, they must be completely honest, repent of all sins, and willing to be set free.

People are not delivered from demons:

If they do not repent of their sins (e.g. Adultery, Abortion, Pornography, etc.)

If they fail to break with the occult.

If they have areas of unforgiveness in their life.

If they are not willing to close the doorways, in their life, that give demonic entry.

(4)   Lead the person in a prayer of repentance, salvation, and deliverance, calling upon the name of the Lord.

**Romans 10:13**

(5)   Have faith in the power of Jesus' name and speak directly to the demons, binding them in Jesus' name.

**Matthew 18:18**
**Mark 3:27**

Don't allow the demons to speak, or to manifest, or to carry on. BIND them in Jesus' name. This restrains and restricts the demons from operating.

# Setting The Captives Free

**PERSONAL NOTES**

"I BIND YOU FROM SPEAKING."

"I BIND YOU FROM MANIFESTING, IN JESUS' NAME."

Jesus, in His ministry, never had conversations or counselling sessions with demons. He said two things: "SHUT UP and COME OUT!"

(6)   Cast the spirits out of the person IN JESUS' NAME.

**Mark 16:17**

**Acts 16:18**

Demons understand, hear, and respond to authority, not volume.

Speak to the demons and command them out in Jesus' name; e.g. arthritis, deafness, infirmity, unclean spirits, witchcraft, etc.

COMMAND the demons not to re-enter.

**Mark 9:25**

(7)   Give the delivered person instructions and Scriptures from God's Word on how to stay delivered and how to resist the devil.

**John 8:31, 32, 36**

**Matthew 12:43-45**

**Ephesians 4:27**

• The one who has been delivered has the responsibility to CLOSE EVERY DOOR to Satan and to fill themselves with God's Word and God's Spirit.

## Demon Spirits and Deliverance - A List of Key Scriptures

| | |
|---|---|
| Matthew 4:23, 24 | Matthew 12:43-45 |
| John 14:12 | Mark 1:23-27 |
| Mark 1:32-34, 39 | Mark 16:17 |
| Luke 9:1, 2 | Luke 10:17-20 |
| Acts 5:15, 16 | Acts 8:5-7 |
| Acts 10:38 | Acts 16:16-18 |
| Acts 19:11-20 | 1 Corinthians 12:10 |
| Ephesians 4:26, 27 | Ephesians 6:10-13 |
| 1 Timothy 4:1, 2 | 2 Timothy 1:7 |
| James 4:7 | 1 John 4:1-4 |
| Revelation 12:11 | |

IMPORTANT: *This week, review your study notes in these two vital lessons and make the decision to take your place in God's army, aggressively destroying the works of the devil and freeing the captives.*

# Response To Truth
*Lessons 11 and 12*

**PERSONAL NOTES**

## KEY QUESTIONS:

(1) What are six of the divine weapons of warfare that belong to us?

(2) How does one recognize demonic influence and activity? Explain.

(3) What revelation knowledge did the early church have about the devil and demons?

(4) How can we protect ourselves from demon spirits?

(5) What are the five things we must know to win in spiritual warfare?

(6) How did Jesus Christ deal with demon spirits?

## MEMORY WORK:

2 Corinthians 10:3-5

James 4:7

Luke 10:19

## PERSONAL APPLICATION:

(1) Write down the seven most important revelation truths that have given you personal insight into the reality of demon spirits.

(2) What will you do with this knowledge? Use or lose it?

(3) Look for ways to share these truths with other people, especially the oppressed, sick, and those needing ministry.

## RECOMMENDED READING:

Rick Godwin, *To Hell With the Devil*

Ray McCauley, *Getting the Devil Off Your Back*

Larry Lea, *The Weapons of Your Warfare*

Kenneth E. Hagin, *The Name of Jesus*